ADELAIDE CRAPSEY

On the life & work
of an American master

ISBN: 978-0-9970994-0-9

Published by Pleiades Press & *Gulf Coast*

Department of English   Department of English
University of Central Missouri   University of Houston
Warrensburg, Missouri 64093   Houston, Texas 77204

Distributed by Small Press Distribution (SPD) and to
subscribers of *Pleiades: Literature in Context* and
Gulf Coast: A Journal of Literature and Fine Arts.

Series, cover, and interior design by Martin Rock.
Cover photograph courtesy of the University of Rochester.

2 4 6 8 9 7 5 3 1
First Printing, 2018

The Unsung Masters Series brings the work of great, out-of-print, little-known writers to new readers. Each volume in the series includes a large selection of the author's original writing, as well as essays on the writer, interviews with people who knew the writer, photographs, and ephemera. The curators of the Unsung Masters Series are always interested in suggestions for future volumes. To suggest a subject, visit UnsungMasters.org.

Invaluable financial support for this project has been provided by the National Endowment for the Arts, the Cynthia Woods Mitchell Center for the Arts, and the Missouri Arts Council, a state agency. Our immense gratitude to these organizations.

ADELAIDE CRAPSEY

On the life & work of an American master

Edited by Jenny Molberg and Christian Bancroft

OTHER BOOKS IN THE UNSUNG MASTERS SERIES

THE UNSUNG MASTERS SERIES

gulf coast + PLEIADES
A JOURNAL OF LITERATURE AND FINE ARTS   P R E S S

CONTENTS

TRANSLATIONS OF CHEROKEE INCANTATIONS

FROM A STUDY IN ENGLISH METRICS

SELECTED LETTERS

IMAGE GALLERY

ESSAYS ON ADELAIDE CRAPSEY

INTRODUCTION

"I WILL NOT LIE STILL": THE LEGACY OF ADELAIDE CRAPSEY

ADELAIDE CRAPSEY is a poet who, with a wink, trespasses beyond the boundaries of linear time. The first time I read her work was a chance encounter with one of her poems online, and I found myself thinking about it for days. The poem was one of her cinquains, entitled "Amaze":

> I know
> Not these my hands
> And yet I think there was
> A woman like me once had hands
> Like these.[1]

To encounter Crapsey's writing now, a century after her untimely death, is an experience embodied in "Amaze." Her work is near-at-hand, as if she'd not been gone these hundred years. The poems anticipate high Modernism in their near-Imagism and formal innovation, evoke meditation on the relationship between poetry and chronic illness, and harken back to Dickinson's sense of Heft; all the while, Crapsey's work maintains a freshness of voice that seems almost new. Adelaide Crapsey exemplifies, in many ways, Eliot's notion of a poet's coherence with the dead,[2] genius's tendency toward unity, and poetry's ability to "transmute into the immediacy of feeling"[3]—albeit with a better sense of humor than Eliot. Though scholars like Karen Alkalay-Gut and Susan Sutton Smith brought Crapsey back into view in the late twentieth century, her work should be more visible in the literary world. Thus, we have gathered a selection of her poems, translations, and letters, a segment of her thesis on prosody, new scholarly essays on her work, and a folio of photographs and artifacts to shed light on her short but luminescent life.

Born in Brooklyn, New York on September 9, 1878, Crapsey was raised in Rochester, New York, and was the third child and second daughter (in a family of nine children) of Rev. Algernon Sidney Crapsey and Adelaide (née Trowbridge) Crapsey. Rev. Crapsey was a well-read, free-thinking Episcopal minister who left his position as Junior Assistant Minister in the Trinity Parish in Brooklyn Heights shortly after Adelaide was born. He believed that money and social class had played too significant a role in the church's affairs. He was an outspoken proponent of equal rights—in 1901, he delivered his "A Constitutional Defense of the Negro" at St. Luke's Church in Washington, D.C., where he argued for Thoreauvian civil disobedience, encouraging voters to go to the polls despite the danger they may face, so as to amend the Constitution, enfranchising African Americans and ending discrimination.[4] In 1906, Algernon Crapsey was charged with heresy because of sermons that advocated a "scientific, democratic, and socialistic" view on religion and, because he called Jesus "middle-class," arguing against the concept of the divinity of Christ.[5] He later left the church. Adelaide, who attended much of the trial, was significantly influenced by her father's sermons, writings, and beliefs.[6]

Adelaide Crapsey first went to a public school in Rochester before matriculating into Kemper Hall, an Episcopalian women's college preparatory school, in 1893. At Kemper Hall, she took classes in French and Latin, played and refereed basketball, and edited the school magazine. Crapsey graduated as the class valedictorian in

1897, and gave a valedictory address called "The Open Road," in which she encouraged "the tradition of the 'wandering spirit' of man, in the name of science, humanity, and adventure."[7] Afterwards, she enrolled at Vassar College, where she was voted Phi Beta Kappa—the first Phi Beta Kappa program at any woman's college.[8] In addition to being the Class Poet for three years, she was the editor-in-chief of the *Vassarion* and managed the basketball team. She wrote stories and poems for the Vassar *Miscellany*, served on the debate team, and wrote and appeared in several plays. Her roommate, "best friend and literary comrade," Jean Webster (to whom letters in this collection are addressed), was the grandniece of Mark Twain, and later wrote the novel *Daddy-Long-Legs*.[9]

Crapsey graduated from Vassar in 1901 with honors and spent a year at home before returning to Kemper Hall to teach history and literature for two years. At Kemper, she experienced the fatigue that would increase over time, before her death from tuberculosis at the age of thirty-six in 1914.

Adelaide Crapsey was funny, tenacious, and willful, especially when dealing with her illness. Her sense of humor, her mischievousness, and her intellectual ambition and curiosity are evidenced in her letters and essays, as well as her characteristic difficulty with spelling, which some biographers have attributed to a learning disability.[10] She is also remembered for her distinctive style, both in poetics and dress—she refused to wear a corset, and she chose mostly monochromatic clothing. Later, this evolved into a wardrobe of almost entirely grey clothing, one mirrored in the dress of her doctor at Saranac Lake, Dr. Baldwin. In one of her letters in this collection, she writes, "Its [*sic*] a great relief to me to find that he is as careful about his greys as I am. Grey overcoat, grey other things, grey tie and a scarf pin of some cloudy grey crystal— All of this I am sure will be a great help."[11]

Crapsey, when remembered, is most often celebrated for her invention of the cinquain, a five-line form that consists of lines of two syllables, then four, six, eight, and two. It is important to note that this is not simply a syllabic form, but a metrical one, as the lines in the cinquain are nearly always iambic. This is evident in "Amaze," or poems like "Night Winds" and "Triad." Crapsey's biographer Karen Alkalay-Gut puts it well when she writes that among the implications of the cinquain "the strongest is that of expanding and curtailed growth, like the life of the poet itself."[12] The sprawl of the fourth line and the strain of the fifth in the cinquain engenders a sense of sudden loss, an anxiety that Crapsey struggled with in her own sense of impending death, and yet the lushness of the fourth line reads as a celebration of life. Even in the darkest days of her illness, which Crapsey was often embarrassed by, she resisted lack of productivity and weakness. This is evident in cinquains in this collection like "Madness" and "Snow," and even more directly in her tour de force, "To the Dead in the Grave-Yard Under My Window":

> Oh, have you no rebellion in your bones?
> Better it is to walk, to run, to dance,
> Better it is to laugh and leap and sing,
> To know the open skies of dawn and night,
> To move untrammel'd down the flaming noon,
> And I will clamour it through weary days
> Keeping the edge of deprivation sharp.
> Nor with the pliant speaking on my lips
> Of resignation, sister to defeat.
> I'll not be patient. I will not lie still.[13]

After Crapsey's graduation from Vassar, she travelled to Europe, where she spent some time in Rome. She studied Keats, and visited his grave, but she did so less with a sense of doom and more as "an empathetic observer."[14] Upon her return to the United States in 1911, she went directly to Smith College, where she taught courses in poetics. There, she met her dear friend, confidant, and intellectual counterpart Esther Lowenthal, to whom some of the letters in this collection are addressed. Crapsey's health quickly deteriorated, though, and she was forced to depart to Saranac Lake, a mountain town with a health facility in the Adirondacks, where she was to spend her last days. Her poems' relationship with illness is a fraught yet inventive one, as in "Lines Addressed to My Left Lung Inconveniently Enamored of Plant Life":

> It was, my lung, most strange of you,
> A freak I cannot pardon,
> Thus to transform yourself into
> A vegetable garden.[15]

Upon deeper exploration of her work, I find it is important to think of Crapsey outside the context of her illness and the poetics of tuberculosis. In fact, it is difficult to categorize Crapsey's poetry, as it anticipates Modernism, but does not embody it; it deals with illness and inevitable death, but does not rely on it as an aesthetic tool. As Erin Adair-Hodges writes in her essay in this collection:

> It does not take away from Crapsey's artistry or unique voice to say she worked within the tradition of her time and place in her treatment of humanity's, and therefore poetry's, primary concerns. It can, however, help us appreciate the notable departures from her presentation of Universal Death, variances which give us a peek into the emergence of a singular poetic voice.

Crapsey died at Saranac Lake, New York on October 8, 1914. After her death, Crapsey's work was celebrated by poets and critics like Carl Sandburg and Yvor Winters, who argued for more visibility of her entire oeuvre. Winters called her a "minor poet of great distinction," and criticized anthologists who ignored her best work, instead always anthologizing the same few cinquains.[16] While many of her cinquains are fascinating, her larger body of work, ranging from a study of the English metric as well as translations from Cherokee incantations, allows us a deeper look into the mind of a brilliant, innovative poet who was both of her time and ahead of it. "Wouldst thou find my ashes?" Crapsey writes in "Immortal

Residue," a poem that captures the project of this collection, " . . . Look / In the pages of my book; / And as these thy hand doth turn, / Know here is my funeral urn."[17]

—Jenny Molberg

NOTES

1 "Amaze," Box 2, File 4, Adelaide Crapsey Papers 1878-1934, The University of Rochester's Rare Books, Special Collections and Preservation, University of Rochester Libraries.

2 Eliot, T.S. "Tradition and the Individual Talent." In *The Sacred Wood: Essays on Poetry and Criticism* (New York: Alfred A. Knopf, 1921), 44.

3 Eliot, T.S. *The Varieties of Metaphysical Poetry: The Clark Lectures at Trinity College and the Turnbull Lectures at the Johns Hopkins University* (San Diego: Harcourt, 1994), 52-3.

4 Alkalay-Gut, Karen. *Alone in the Dawn: The Life of Adelaide Crapsey* (Athens: University of Georgia Press, 1988), 112.

5 Ibid, 148.

6 Ibid, 145-169.

7 Ibid, 62.

8 Ibid, 105.

9 The Vassar Encyclopedia. "Adelaide Crapsey." Accessed May 15, 2017. http://vcencyclopedia.vassar.edu/alumni/adelaide-crapsey.html.

10 Alkalay-Gut, Karen. *Alone in the Dawn: The Life of Adelaide Crapsey* (Athens: University of Georgia Press, 1988), 59.

11 Adelaide Crapsey to Esther Lowenthal, 2 October 1913, Box 1, Folder 7, Adelaide Crapsey Papers 1878-1934, The University of Rochester's Rare Books, Special Collections and Preservation, University of Rochester Libraries.

12 Alkalay-Gut, Karen. *Alone in the Dawn: The Life of Adelaide Crapsey* (Athens: University of Georgia Press, 1988), 9.

13 "To the Dead in The Grave-Yard Under My Window," *The Complete Poems and Collected Letters of Adelaide Crapsey*, ed. Susan Sutton Smith (Albany: State University of New York Press, 1977), 229.

14 Ibid, 210.

15 "Lines Addressed to My Left Lung Inconveniently Enamoured of Plant-Life," Box 2, File 1, Adelaide Crapsey Papers 1878-1934, The University of Rochester's Rare Books, Special Collections and Preservation, University of Rochester Libraries.

16 Smith, Susan Sutton. "Adelaide Crapsey: 'An Unconscious Imagist,'" *University of Rochester Library Bulletin*, no. 37 (1984), n.p.

17 "Immortal Residue," Box 2, File 4, Adelaide Crapsey Papers 1878-1934, The University of Rochester's Rare Books, Special Collections and Preservation, University of Rochester Libraries.

"CAN YOU READ THE HORRID SCRAWL": ON THE ARCHIVES OF ADELAIDE CRAPSEY

CRAPSEY was something of an archivist with all of her work on prosody and many drafts of material for her *A Study of English Metrics*. Her syllabic tallying—especially as it pertains to her own poems—is meticulously recorded. Exploring the archives at Rochester, one can look, for instance, at the hundreds of slips from the British Museum cataloguing the books that Crapsey checked out during her stay in London from 1909-1910. As expected, she checked out a large number of books written by and on Milton, Keats, and other canonical poets. More intriguing moments in these slips record Crapsey's foray into Charles Baudelaire's *Les Fleurs du Mal* or George Santayana's *The Sense of Beauty*. Though her reading of these poets does not seem to play a salient role in her critical work, it does reveal their influence on her poetry. It would be remiss, then, to present the collection of her work in this volume without addressing the archival material at Rochester.

The University of Rochester's Rare Books, Special Collections and Preservation Department houses the Adelaide Crapsey Papers in Rochester, New York. The four boxes located there are almost all teeming with scrapbooks, letters, poetry and criticism drafts, photos, newspaper clippings, and musical scores that were inspired by her poetry. Many of the documents that we now have access to are thanks to Crapsey's family and Esther Lowenthal, a colleague and supporter of Crapsey's at Smith College. The University of Rochester began receiving papers from Crapsey's family in 1961, specifically from her brother Paul B. Crapsey; Lowenthal gave papers in 1961, 1965, and 1966; Arthur H. Crapsey, Jr. donated papers in 1970; and John S. Marsh donated archival material in 1978. During that time and since then, the library has made various purchases also contributing to the Adelaide Crapsey Papers.

The number of published works on Crapsey peaked around the same time, with Susan Sutton Smith's edition of *The Complete Poems & Collected Letters of Adelaide Crapsey*,[1] Edward Butscher's short biography *Adelaide Crapsey*,[2] and Hideo Kawanami's important work drawing correlations between Crapsey's poetry and Japanese poetry. 1988 saw the publication of Karen Alkalay-Gut's biography *Alone in the Dawn: The Life of Adelaide Crapsey*[3]. Since then, the amount of scholarship on Crapsey has diminished significantly. In 2014, however, an anthology of women modernist poets, edited by Robert Haas and Paul Ebenkamp, was released by Counterpoint Press, and featured a number of poems by Crapsey, most notably her cinquains.

With the advent of new Modernist studies at the beginning of the twenty-first century, we can only hope that this volume contributes to that pedigree, which in part attempts to reframe Modernist studies through other considerations such as gender politics. The gendered nature of Modernist studies clearly displays its biases since it has not already publicized the work of Modernist female writers like Crapsey. While some of the materials at Rochester have been published, like Crapsey's poems and letters in Smith's edited collection, other aspects of the archives have not been discussed as thoroughly, like her work on translation, which has received little-to-no attention. Her illness, similarly, has been mentioned in biographies, but not really in the context of Crapsey as a woman subjected to the sexist assumptions and treatments of doctors during the early twentieth century.

Virtually every document at Rochester has a reason for its place in the archives. Even what seems to be trivial at first (like the many drafts and redrafts of *A Study of English Metrics*) has its purpose. Crapsey's scrapbook alone, located in Box 1, contains a wealth of information chronicled across her short life and would provide any scholar with enough information to fill a small tome. For a poet as under-recognized as Crapsey, the amount of material at Rochester is impressive. There is certainly less material available for other people in archives around the world. Despite this, a researcher always wishes there were just a little bit more—one scrap of explanation as to why Crapsey decided to translate Cherokee charms or something more personal, like whether she ever had a lover.

Anybody perusing Crapsey's letters already aware of her untimely death would become a little *verklempt* at the languid progression of her illness, knowing too well that none of the treatments prescribed by Dr. Edward Baldwin worked. Meanwhile, Crapsey, though clearly frustrated with her situation, never appeared to grow irate or depressed. In her letters, she laments her almost constant state of exhaustion, but spends just as much time apologizing about the state of her handwriting or tardy responses.

Most touching, perhaps, are the letters that the Crapseys received after Adelaide's passing and the general outpouring of affection to her after the publication of *Verse* in 1918. Even Harriett Monroe, the Editor of *Poetry*, noted after Crapsey's death:

> Adelaide Crapsey, dying at thirty-six in 1914 used her art like a sword to defend herself bitterly against the threatening enemy. Frail and aloof, she wrote of the fullness and glory of life, of Birth Moment and the Mother Exultant. From her deathbed she uttered, to "the dead in the graveyard" under her window, a fierce protest against their sordid lives . . . .And so, "mistily radiant," she was led off by the conqueror—but not to utter silence and darkness, for the shadowed fire of her spirit

burns on with singular intensity in her small book of tragic but exultant song.[4]

Monroe's associate editor, Alice Corbin Henderson, wrote a more sober, though erroneous, review in *Poetry*, claiming that it was "hard to separate Adelaide Crapsey's poems from the circumstances of her death, as recorded in the brief preface by a friend."[5] Henderson's review was provoked by letters from Carl Sandburg, a fellow Chicago poet: "From Adelaide Crapsey's book I get much of the repression, the reticences, and the quivering color points of your work. Have you seen the book?"[6] Sandburg also told Henderson, "Your New Mexico songs are hauntingly beautiful. Your groups in back numbers of *Poetry* have for me the same irreducible glimmer that there is to Adelaide Crapsey's work and when you cash in if I don't write a better obituary for you than I did for Adelaide I'm guessing wrong."[7]

The researcher, nonetheless, is to act as an agent for future generations, to spotlight material from the archives and build on the information that already exists using that material. Due to their incomplete and ever-changing states, archives tend to raise more questions than they can answer. The researcher, therefore, must draw attention to any gaps, proposing hypotheses about what they might signify, and, more importantly, why we should care. In this sense, the researcher acts as a deconstructionist and a reconstructionist of documents, histories, and the people in those histories. This is not to say that the researcher represents some amalgamation of an Indiana Jones figure and a forensic scientist from *Law and Order*. The researcher, of course, must adhere to a code of ethics. The collage of information that they come across must be decoded and presented to the larger public under logical premises. Thus, a passage in a letter Crapsey sent to her mother about protesting corsets might be a source used to argue the feminist principles that she upheld. Likewise, the scattered pieces of information from letters and ephemera on home and herbal remedies raise the possibility that Crapsey knew a thing or two about homeopathy.

Most of the letters in the Crapsey papers are written by Crapsey. However, this presents two difficulties: 1) her handwriting can be very difficult to read; 2) and her spelling is abysmal. Fortunately, most of the letters have been typed by the university, though there are a number of places throughout her epistolary correspondence where words or phrases are left blank because of her spelling or her handwriting. With other documents, like her drafts of *A Study of English Metrics*, she writes much more legibly (and her spelling is accurate). As shown in the figure below, her scrupulous way of a drawing tables and calculating statistics is so clear, it makes one wonder why all of her letters couldn't be written as legibly. Of course, the answer to this is simple: she was composing drafts for her book to be sent out to publishers for publication.

Crapsey worked on *A Study of English Metrics* for over a decade, originally titling it "An Experiment on English Prosody." From 1902 through the middle of 1913, she prioritized her work for this book above her poetry.[8] Upon looking inside it, the scrupulous attention to prosodic detail in the work of English poets is undeniable. She constructed graphs and tables that displayed the number of words in books like *Paradise Lost* and Tennyson's "Ulysses," calculating the percent of monosyllables, disyllables, and polysyllables, as in the following:

TABLE III.

TENNYSON	Total No. of words	Per cent Mono-disyllable	Per cent Polysyllable
Oenone.................	1,988	94.31	5.68
Ulysses................	556	96.94	3.05
Tithonus...............	599	96.33	3.67
The Coming of Arthur...	4,256	96.54	3.45
Merlin and Vivien......	7,896	95.88	4.10
Lancelot and Elaine.....	11,799	95.83	4.15
The Holy Grail.........	7,474	96.48	3.50
Guinevere..............	5,671	95.68	4.30
The Passing of Arthur...	3,855	96.59	3.39

Figure 1[9]

The numerous drafts of *A Study of English Metrics* at the Rochester archives is an impressive addition to the collection. One can see the steady progression to her final draft from the initial study in prosody that she began years earlier. As you move closer to her final draft, the differences between them become hardly noticeable. The amount of time that she spent counting syllables and calculating percentages in books as long as *Paradise Lost*, not to mention writing and rewriting the tables for these calculations, becomes quite astonishing.

One particularly interesting document in the archives pertaining to her metrical studies is a letter she received from W.G. Howard, a secretary at the Modern Language Association. The letter, dated September 30, 1914, is a rejection of her submission of an essay from the previous June. Based on the way Howard prefaces the rejection, it seems possible that Crapsey may have sent another letter after her initial one, inquiring into the state of her submission. "If you feel that the Modern Language Association has been very neglectful of your interests,"[10] Howard begins, "I do not wonder, and I must confess to a certain sense of humility, though our delay in sending you word with reference to your article has come about thru no fault of mine." He goes on to blame the "scattering of academicians at the end of academic year" and "the European war to boot" for the delay in his response.

Given that roughly three months had passed since Crapsey sent out her essay, the September response is not too unusual. Since it appears that Crapsey inquired before the September 30th date, she seems especially eager to get published. In her biography of Crapsey, Alkalay-Gut tells us that "the last two months at Saranac Lake brought scattered attempts at creativity,"[11] which included attempts on behalf of Webster to submit Crapsey's collection, *Verse*, for publication. Like anyone else who reads Crapsey's study, the editors at MLA likewise noted the "scrupulous accuracy of [her] labors." The letter continues by adding that "we do not see that you hav [*sic*] arrived at results which may be cald [*sic*] commensurate with the labors, and which your method may hav [sic] in store for the future." A letter from October 15, 1914, written by Lowenthal, reads:

> My dear Mr. Howard,
>
> I have your letter of September 30 to Miss Crapsey relative to her paper on metrics. Miss Crapsey had prepared a further paper which I think shows the metrical application of the analysis she submitted to you. There are besides other papers left incomplete at Miss Crapsey's death on October eighth. It falls to me with a very inadequate equipment, to put these papers together when I shall have made a tentative arrangement, may I take advantage of your kind offer of interest and send the papers to you?
>
> Perhaps you can tell me of some one [sic] whose special work lies in the field of English prosody?
>
> Faithfully yours,
>
> Esther Lowenthal[12]

Based on Lowenthal's response, it's not entirely clear if Crapsey saw Howard's response on September 30. The paper that she "had prepared" was unlikely to have been written between the receipt of Howard's letter and the time of her death.

In a letter dated September 25, 1913, Crapsey tells her mother, Adelaide Crapsey (née Trowbridge), that she hoped to recover soon at Saranac Lake to "get at the metrical stuff in ernest [sic] soon—even to the extent of tackling the 2d paper after I get this one off to the Modern Language Review—But of course I'll be guided—well mainly by my pulse, I suppose—how silly!"[13] In addition, by this time, Dr. Baldwin had advised Crapsey not to work on her metrical project, so as not to tire her. Before Crapsey even sent her project to MLA, she sent a draft of her metrical study to *The Nation* on June 20, 1913. In it, she address Paul Elmer More, acknowledging that her essay is not the kind of material published by *The Nation*:

> It is not, I know, usual for *The Nation* to publish a paper of the sort I am forwarding to you yet I send it on the bare chance that you may perhaps consider it. It is, as you can see, a study in English verse-technique and after a good deal of rather rueful wondering I am still able to think only of you and perhaps Mr Irving-Babbitt as at all likely to be interested in this sort of work it represents. And, indeed, whether you find it available for *The Nation* or not, it would be to me the greatest pleasure if you would read it. There are only forty-two pages and the conclusions, if they will hold, are I think important enough to be interesting.
>
> If I am not other [?] frankly and anxiously concerned over the matter of publication it is because I can see no other way in which to bring the matter under discussion—working alone is always dangerous—and because it may be a first step toward gaining the free time that detailed investigation of this kind really demands.
>
> I am sorry to send the paper just on the edge of summer but I work subject to such constant interruption that I have not been able to finish it earlier as I had hoped to do.[14]

Of course, Crapsey's essay was not picked up for publication in *The Nation*. Although the archives do not have More's reply to Crapsey, there is a letter to Lowenthal, dated July 17, 1913, in which Crapsey does not express any surprise at More's response to her submission:

> I finished the favorite literature [her name for the prosody essay] and sent it on Saturday the 21st of June. I reckoned that it would take P.E.M. about 3 weeks to get around to reading his surprise and settled back to rest during that time. It came back on Tuesday the 23rd ... The thing was too long for the Nation

but I seem to have "hit on a very interesting point"—but the argument was hard to follow (E! that masterpiece of lucidity!)[15]

More's response did ask Crapsey to resubmit a condensed version of the essay, but it's not evident what became of that version after she resent it. While these submission letters do not seem valuable at first glance, additions like these in the archives contribute to our understanding of Crapsey's faith in her own work, her interaction with publishers (because after her death, Lowenthal was the primary executor of her poetry and criticism), and the timeline by which she sent material out before her passing. Crapsey's letter to *The Nation* displays her self-consciousness as well as her self-effacing behavior about her work as a scholar. This, however, might provide insight into the relationship between women and the publishing industry in the early twentieth century. Her trepidations concern themselves with the kind of material that *The Nation* usually publishes, which is to say, she does not believe that her work is even valuable—if her theories "will hold," she says. Nonetheless, Crapsey's uncertainty regarding the state of her health makes its way into this letter as well. While she is "sorry to send the paper just on the edge of summer," she is only too aware of the "constant interruption[s]" in her life that prevent her from spending more time on her prosodic study.

As indicated in her letter, Lowenthal claims that the burden rests on her to sift through Crapsey's drafts and notes to present them to prospective publishers. Here, as elsewhere, the archives reveal how much work and dedication Lowenthal put into Crapsy's legacy. Though the full extent of their relationship can only be glimpsed by the letters exchanged between the two women, they do suggest the trust that Crapsey placed in Lowenthal—not just as a friend, but as a colleague. In their correspondence, Crapsey confesses such quotidian information as experiencing pain while getting out of bed or her pneumothorax treatment while under the care of Dr. Baldwin. "On the 8th of July as I got out of my bath,"[16] Crapsey writes from the same July 13th letter as the one described above, "I leaned over quickly felt a remarkable pain and after a second found it more discrete [*sic*] to drop full length on the bathroom floor than to stand up."[17] These moments, while they seemed to Crapsey "awfully funny . . . and nothing at all serious," read as a little tragic. After visiting the doctor, she was advised to stay in a hospital for three or four weeks to rest. Crapsey claimed that she didn't like updating Lowenthal about her health. She always "[felt] like an idiot" when talking about symptoms. Moments such as these—though seemingly insignificant—clarify a number of aspects in Crapsey's life that the archives don't otherwise explicitly reveal.

Almost all of the scholarship devoted to Crapsey ties her to Modernism. Scholars like Alkalay-Gut do not unequivocally call her a high Modernist, but Crapsey's imagistic cinquains certainly draw parallels to Imagism and other early twentieth-century literatures. The more important question to raise is not why her work relate to Modernism, but in what ways Crapsey has a connection with Modernism. One piece of evidence exists in the Crapsey-Lowenthal correspondence, dated May 16, 1914. In the letter to Lowenthal, Crapsey encloses a 1914 advertisement for *BLAST*, the short-lived literary magazine affiliated with the Vorticist movement in Britain. Crapsey does not tell Lowenthal where she heard about *BLAST*, only writing on the advertisement clipping: "Rather delightful, dont [*sic*] you think so—We must have it! I'll order it + have it for your entertainment."[18] Crapsey's enthusiasm for the literary magazine makes apparent her familiarity with current literary culture. She also read the monthly issues of *Poetry* and the *Atlantic* —"when," according to Alkalay-Gut, "she had the strength."[19] There can be no doubt, then, that she was aware of the innovations occurring at the time in poetry.

The archives also contain several drafts of her own poetry, for which she counts syllables and metrical beats, indicated by tiny numbers written throughout the documents. There is one standout example in the archives of her cinquain "Snow,"[21] which, scribbled over the course of a couple pages, tracks the progress of the poem from inception to completion. Below a draft of "Nor moon," are fits and starts of "Snow" that begin:

> Look up,
> O sage, the wi,
> Look up,
> The earliest wind
> of winter,

and another:

> Look up
> With sudden breath
> the keen, and wintry wind.

Yet another draft—this time, titled as "The Snow!"—is written:

> Look up,
> the first light breath,
> ~~greeted of wintry wind~~
> ~~blows from the hills . . . look up and scent~~
> ~~The snow!~~[22]

Compared to the first attempts at the poem, the physical act of looking at the snow is depicted more clearly in the final draft. Adjectives like "earliest wind" and "keen . . . wind" do not add anything to the terseness in which Crapsey's poetics engage. If anything, they convolute the poem's action. Furthermore, moments like "O sage" in the drafts incorporate unnecessary additions to the poem, removing it from its focus, which is entirely on the phenomenological reaction to snow materializing "From the bleakening hills."

Another poem that takes up the same season, "Winter," appears on the page previous to "Snow," and what's striking about their proximity is the dramatic shift in tone from one poem to the other.

Unlike the innocent delight in snowfall in "Snow," "Winter" depicts this grim scene of a blizzard that threatens the people who live nearby. The first draft is as follows:

> The cold
> with steely grip
> clutches the land in alack
> the little people in the hills
> will die![23]

The only difference between the rough and final drafts is the change of "grip" to "clutches." The sonic and rhythmic nature of the second line makes "clutches" a much better match than "grip." Although Crapsey's work was not averse to bleak subject matter, as exhibited in a number of cinquains like "Release," "Trapped," and "Madness," these two poems above, likely written in the same sitting, call attention to Crapsey's tonal range, even if the poems address similar subjects.

Other aspects of the Crapsey Papers reveal her meticulous way of measuring syllables and meter in her poems. For example, a drafts of poems like "What News, Comrades" and "Tears," show the diacritical marks above words to denote phonetic stresses. Not all of the drafts of her poems are composed with these marks, so it's interesting to think about reasons why she selectively marked the stresses in her poems. One possibility is that Crapsey's research in metrics attuned her ear well enough to the point that she didn't need to track the stresses in every poem. Another, perhaps obvious, reason is that not all of her poetry is written in strict metrical forms. Despite all her formalist work, Crapsey cannot be thought of exclusively as a formalist in the Western sense. Her cinquains are composed of specific syllabic structures, but they also suggest an affinity to Eastern poetic traditions.

Ultimately, what the archive shows is that Crapsey was a meticulous writer—in both her poetry and prose. Even during the moments spent at the lake, she displays an unflinching interest in current movements in literature as well as a dedication to her own literary projects. The evidence of Crapsey's hours of research informs her attention to syllabic and metrical structure in both *A Study of English Metrics* and her own verse. While the work in this book is significant, the Adelaide Crapsey Papers at Rochester indicate that there are still a number of projects on this American master yet to be undertaken.

—Christian Bancroft

NOTES

1   Crapsey, Adelaide. *The Complete Poems & Collected Letters of Adelaide Crapsey.* ed. Susan Sutton Smith (State U of New York P, 1977).

2   Butscher, Edward. *Adelaide Crapsey* (Twayne Publishers, 1979).

3   Alkalay-Gut, Karen. *Alone in the Dawn: The Life of Adelaide Crapsey* (The U of Georgia P, 1988).

4   Monroe, Harriet, *Poets and Their Art* (New York: Macmillan, 1926), 137-38.

5   Henderson, Alice Corben, "The Great Adventure," *Poetry: A Magazine of Verse*, 10 (1917), 317.

6   Sanburg, Carl, *The Letters of Carl Sandburg*, ed. Herbert Mitgang (New York: Harcourt, Brace & World, 1969), 115.

7   Ibid., 124.

8   It was only in late 1913 and early 1914 that she devoted more time to poetry than her criticism, when her doctors were convinced that all of her syllable counting provoked her fragile condition.

9   Crapsey, Adelaide, *A Study of English Metrics*, An Introductory Note by Esther Lowenthal (New York: Knopf, 1918), 23..

10 W.G. Howard to Adelaide Crapsey, 30 September 1914, Box 1, Folder 7, Adelaide Crapsey Papers 1878-1934, The University of Rochester's Rare Books, Special Collections and Preservation, University of Rochester Libraries.

11 Alkalay-Gut, Karen, *Alone in the Dawn: The Life of Adelaide Crapsey* (Athens: U of Georgia P, 1988), 289.

12 Esther Lowenthal to W.G. Howard, 15 September 1914, Box 1, Folder 7, Adelaide Crapsey Papers 1878-1934, The University of Rochester's Rare Books, Special Collections and Preservation, University of Rochester Libraries.

13 Adelaide Crapsey to Adelaide Crapsey (née Trowbridge), 25 September 1913, Box 1, Folder 1, Adelaide Crapsey Papers 1878-1934, The University of Rochester's Rare Books, Special Collections and Preservation, University of Rochester Libraries.

14 Adelaide Crapsey to Paul Elmer More, 20 June 1913, Box 1, Folder 1, Adelaide Crapsey Papers 1878-1934, The University of Rochester's Rare Books, Special Collections and Preservation, University of Rochester Libraries.

15 Adelaide Crapsey to Esther Lowenthal, 17 July 1913, Box 1, Folder 6, Adelaide Crapsey Papers 1878-1934, The University of Rochester's Rare Books, Special Collections and Preservation, University of Rochester Libraries.

16 Adelaide Crapsey to Esther Lowenthal, 3 July 1914, Box 1, Folder 6, Adelaide Crapsey Papers 1878-1934, The University of Rochester's Rare Books, Special Collections and Preservation, University of Rochester Libraries.

17 Ibid.

18 Adelaide Crapsey to Esther Lowenthal, 16 May 1914, Box 1, Folder 5, Adelaide Crapsey Papers 1878-1934, The University of Rochester's Rare Books, Special

Collections and Preservation, University of Rochester Libraries.

19 Alkalay-Gut, Karen, *Alone in the Dawn: The Life of Adelaide Crapsey* (Athens: U of Georgia P, 1988), 277.

20 Adelaide Crapsey, Poems, Drafts of "Nor Moon . . ." and "Snow," Box 2, Folder 2, Adelaide Crapsey Papers 1878-1934, The University of Rochester's Rare Books, Special Collections and Preservation, University of Rochester Libraries.

21 Ibid.

22 Ibid.

A Note about the Text

Due to Crapsey's sometimes indecipherable handwriting and unconventional spelling and punctuation, we have had to make numerous editorial decisions about how her work appears in this volume. We have inserted clarifying remarks in brackets where those seem necessary to avoid confusion. Throughout, we have opted to reproduce Crapsey's misspellings and unusual uses of punctuation to retain the idiosyncrasy of her voice. Therefore, where idiosyncracies of punctuation or spelling occur, the reader can be confident that these have been reproduced from the original manuscripts.

SELECTED POEMS

Birth-Moment

Behold her,
Running through the waves,
Eager to reach the land;
The water laps her,
Sun and wind are on her,
Healthy, brine-drenched and young,
Behold Desire new-born;—
Desire on first fulfillment's radiant edge,
Love at miraculous moment of emergence,
This is she,
Who running,
Hastens, hastens to the land.

Look. . Look. .
Her blown gold hair and lucent eyes of youth,
Her body rose and ivory in the sun. .
Look,
How she hastens,
Running, running to the land.

Her hands are yearning and her feet are swift
To reach and hold
She knows not what
Yet knows that it is life;
Need urges her,
Self, uncomprehending but most deep divined,
Unwilled but all-compelling, drives her on.
Life runs to life.
She who longs,

But hath not yet accepted or bestowed,
All virginal dear and bright,
Runs, runs to reach the land.

And she who runs shall be
Married to blue of summer skies at noon,
Companion to green fields,
Held bride of subtle fragrance and of all sweet sound,
Beloved of the stars,
And wanton mistress to the veering winds.

Oh breathless space between:
Womb-time just passed,
Dark-hidden, chaotic-formative, unpersonal,
And individual life of fresh-created force
Not yet begun:
One moment more
Before desire shall meet desire
And new creation start.
Oh breathless space,
While she,
Just risen from the waves,
Runs, runs to reach the land.

(Ah, keenest personal moment
When mouth unbiased turns eager-slow and tremulous
Towards lover's mouth,
That tremulous and eager-slow
Droops down to it:

But breathless space of breath or two
Lies in between
Before the mouth upturned and mouth down-drooped
Shall meet and make the kiss.)

Look. . Look. .
She runs. .
Love fresh-emerged,
Desire new-born. .
Blown on by wind,
And shone on by the sun,
She rises from the waves
And running,
Hastens, hastens to the land.
Beloved and Beloved and Beloved,
Even so right
And beautiful and undenied
Is my desire;
Even so longing-swift
I run to your receiving arms.

O Aphrodite!
O Aphrodite, hear!
Hear my wrung cry flame upward poignant-glad . . .
This is my time for me.
I too am young;
I too am all of love!

John Keats

(February 1820 – February 1821)

Meet thou the event
And terrible happening of
Thine end: for thou art come
Upon the remote, cold place
Of ultimate dissolution and
With dumb, wide look
Thou, impotent, dost feel
Impotence creeping on
Thy potent soul. Yea, now caught in
The aghast and voiceless pain
Of death, thyself doth watch
Thyself becoming naught,

Peace. . Peace. . For at
The last is comfort. Lo, now
Thou hast no pain. Lo, now
The waited presence is
Within the room; the voice
Speaks final-gentle: "Child,
Even thy careful nurse,
I lift thee in my arms
For greater ease and while
Thy heart still beats, place my
Cool fingers of oblivion on
Thine eyes and close them for
Eternity. Thou shalt
Pass sleeping, nor know
When sleeping ceases. Yet still
A little while thy breathing lasts,

Gradual is faint and fainter; I
Must listen close—the end."

Rest. And you others. . All.
Grave-fellows in
Green place. Here grows
Memorial every spring's
Fresh grass and here
Your marking monument
Was built for you long, long
Ago when Caius Cestius died.

Rome 1909.

November Night

Listen . . .
With faint dry sound,
Like steps of passing ghosts,
The leaves, frost-crisp'd, break from the trees
And fall.

Release

With swift
Great sweep of her
Magnificent arm my pain
Clanged back the doors that shut my soul
From life.

Triad

These be
Three silent things:
The falling snow . . . the hour
Before the dawn . . . the mouth of one
Just dead.

Snow

Look up . . .
From bleakening hills
Blows down the light, first breath
Of wintry wind . . . look up, and scent
The snow!

Anguish

Keep thou
Thy tearless watch
All night but when blue dawn
Breathes on the silver moon, then weep!
Then weep!

Trapped

Well and
If day on day
Follows, and weary year
On year ... and ever days and years ...
Well?

Moon-Shadows

Still as
On windless nights
The moon-cast shadows are,
So still will be my heart when I
Am dead.

Susanna and the Elders

"Why do
You thus devise
Evil against her?" "For that
She is beautiful, delicate:
Therefore."

Youth

But me
They cannot touch,
Old age and death. . the strange
And ignominious end of old
Dead folk!

Languor After Pain

Pain ebbs,
And like cool balm,
An opiate weariness
Settles on eye-lids, on relaxed
Pale wrists.

The Guarded Wound

If it
Were lighter touch
Than petal of flower resting
On grass oh still too heavy it were,
Too heavy!

Winter

The cold
With steely clutch
Grips all the land . . . alack,
The little people in the hills
Will die!

Night Winds

The old
Old winds that blew
When chaos was, what do
They tell the clattered trees that I
Should weep?

Arbutus

Not spring's
Thou art, but hers,
Most cool, most virginal,
Winter's, with thy faint breath, thy snows
Rose-tinged.

Roma Aeterna

The sun
Is warm to-day,
O Romulus, and on
Thine olden Palatine the birds
Still sing.

Amaze

I know
Not these my hands
And yet I think there was
A woman like me once had hands
Like these.

Shadow

A-sway,
On red rose,
A golden butterfly. .
And on my heart a butterfly
Night-wing'd.

Madness

Burdock,
Blue aconite,
And thistle and thorn . . . of these,
Singing I wreathe my pretty wreath
O'death.

The Warning

Just now,
Out of the strange
Still dusk. . as strange, as still. .
A white moth flew. Why am I grown
So cold?

Saying of Il Haboul

*Guardian of the Treasure of Solomon
and Keeper of the Prophet's Armour*

My tent
A vapour that
The wind dispels and but
As dust before the wind am I
Myself.

Laurel in the Berkshires

Sea-foam
And coral! Oh, I'll
Climb the great pasture rocks
And dream me mermaid in the sun's
Gold flood.

Niagara

Seen on a night in November

How frail
Above the bulk
Of crashing water hangs,
Autumnal, evanescent, wan,
The moon.

The Grand Canyon

By Zeus!
Shout word of this
To the eldest dead! Titans,
Gods, Heroes, come who have once more
A home!

Now Barabbas Was a Robber

No guile?
Nay, but so strangely
He moves among us. . Not this
Man but Barabbas! Release to us
Barabbas!

On Seeing Weather-Beaten Trees

Is it as plainly in our living shown,
By slant and twist, which way the wind hath blown?

The Entombment

In a cave born,
(Mary said)
In a cave is
My Son burièd.

Narcissus

"Boy, lying
Where the long grass
Edges the pool's brim,
What do you watch
There in the water? the blue
Colour of Heaven
Mirrored, repeated? the brown
Tree-trunks and branches
Waveringly imaged? These,
Boy, do you watch?"
"Nay but mine eyes;
Nay but the trouble
Deep in mine eyes."

Pierrot

For Aubrey Beardsley's picture "Pierrot is dying."

Pierrot is dying;
    Tiptoe in,
Finger touched to lip,
    Harlequin,
Columbine and Clown.

Hush! how still he lies
    In his bed,
White slipped hand and white
    Sunken head.
Oh, poor Pierrot.

There's his dressing-gown
    Across the chair,
Slippers on the floor . . .
    Can he hear
Us who tiptoe in?

Pillowed high he lies
    In his bed;
Listen, Columbine.
    "He is dead."
Oh, poor Pierrot.

The Monk in the Garden

He comes from Mass early in the morning

The sky's very blue Madonna wears;
   The air's alive with gold! Mark you the way
The birds sing and the dusted shimmer of dew
   On leaf and fruit? . . Per Bacco, what a day!

Night

I have minded me
Of the noon-day brightness,
And the crickets' drowsy
Singing in the sunshine. .

I have minded me
Of the slim marsh-grasses
That the winds at twilight,
Dying, scarcely ripple. .

And I cannot sleep.

I have minded me
Of a lily-pond,
Where the waters sway
All the moonlit leaves
And the curled long stems. .

And I cannot sleep.

Harvesters' Song

Reap, reap the grain and gather
The sweet grapes from the vine;
Our Lord's mother is weeping,
She hath nor bread nor wine;
She is weeping, The Queen of Heaven,
She hath nor breath nor wine.

Mad-Song

Grey gaolers are my griefs
      That will not let me free;
The bitterness of tears
      Is warder unto me.

I may not leap or run;
      I may nor laugh nor sing.
"Thy cell is small," they say,
      "Be still thou captived thing."

But in the dusk of the night,
      Too sudden-swift to see,
Closing and ivory gates
      Are refuge unto me.

My griefs, my tears must watch,
      And cold the watch they keep;
They whisper, whisper there—
      I hear them in my sleep.

They know that I must come,
      And patient watch they keep,
Whispering, shivering there,
      Till I come back from sleep.

But in the dark of a night,
      Too dark for them to see,
The refuge of black gates
      Will open unto me.

Whisper up there in the dark. .
     Shiver by bleak winds stung. .
My dead lips laugh to hear
     How long you wait . . . how long!

Grey gaolers are my griefs
     That will not let me free;
The bitterness and tears
     Is warder unto me.

The Witch

When I was a girl by Nilus stream
    I watched the desert stars arise;
My lover, he who dreamed the Sphinx,
    Learned all his dreaming from my eyes.

I bore in Greece a burning name,
    And I have been in Italy
Madonna to a painter-lad,
    And mistress to a Medici.

And have you heard (and I have heard)
    Of puzzled men with decorous mien,
Who judged—The wench knows far too much—
    And burnt her on the Salem green?

The Lonely Death

In the cold I will rise, I will bathe
In waters of ice; myself
Will shiver, and shrive myself,
Alone in the dawn, and anoint
Forehead and feet and hands;
I will shutter the windows from light,
I will place in their sockets the four
Tall candles and set them a-flame
In the grey of the dawn; and myself
Will lay myself straight in my bed,
And draw the sheet under my chin.

The Immortal Residue

Inscription for my verse

Wouldst thou find my ashes? Look
In the pages of my book;
And as these thy hand doth turn,
Know here is my funeral urn.

To the Dead in the Grave-Yard Under My Window

—Written in A Moment of Exasperation

How can you lie so still? All day I watch
And never a blade of all the green sod moves
To show where restlessly you toss and turn,
And fling a desperate arm or draw up knees
Stiffened and aching from their long disuse;
I watch all night and not one ghost comes forth
To take its freedom of the midnight hour.
Oh, have you no rebellion in your bones?
The very worms must scorn you where you lie,
A pallid moldering acquiescent folk,
Meek habitants of unresented graves.
Why are you there in your straight row on row
Where I must ever see you from my bed
That in your mere dumb presence iterate
The text so weary in my ears: "Lie still
And rest; be patient and lie still and rest."
I'll not be patient! I will not lie still!
There is a brown road runs between the pines,
And further on the purple woodlands lie,
And still beyond blue mountains lift and loom;
And I would walk the road and I would be
Deep in the wooded shade and I would reach
The windy mountain tops that touch the clouds.
My eyes may follow but my feet are held.
Recumbent as you others must I too
Submit? Be mimic of your movelessness
With pillow and counter pane for stone and sod?
And if the many sayings of the wise

Teach of submission I will not submit
But with a spirit all unreconciled
Flash an unquenched defiance to the stars.
Better it is to walk, to run, to dance,
Better it is to laugh and leap and sing,
To know the open skies of dawn and night,
To move untrammel'd down the flaming noon,
And I will clamour it through weary days
Keeping the edge of deprivation sharp.
Nor with the pliant speaking on my lips
Of resignation, sister to defeat.
I'll not be patient. I will not lie still.

And in ironic quietude who is
The despot of our days and lord of dust
Needs but, scarce heeding, wait to drop
Grim casual comment on rebellion's end:
"Yes, yes . . . Wilful and petulant but now
As dead and quiet as the others are."
And this each body and ghost of you hath heard
That in your graves do therefore lie so still.

To an Unfaithful Lover

What words
Are left thee then
Who hast squandered on thy
Forgetfulness eternity's
I love?

Untitled

Why have
I thought the dew
Ephemeral when I
Shall rest so short a time, myself,
On earth?

Lunatick.

Dost thou
Not feel them slip,
How cold! how cold! the moon's
Thin wavering finger-tips, along
Thy throat?

Sad of Heart

Thou beautiful and ivory gates
    That shut my tears away from me—
Even, at last, such refuge yield
    The great, safe doors of Ebony.

Epigram

If illness' end be health regained then I
Will pay you, Asculapeus, when I die.

Incantation

O mia luna! Porta mi fortuna!
(You must say it nine times, curtseying, and then wish.)

In rose, pale, fading blue of twilight sky,
    See, the new moon's thin crescent shining clear;
Nine times I'll curtsey murmuring mystic words,—
    And wish good fortune to our love, my dear.

Lines Addressed to my Left Lung Inconveniently Enamoured of Plant-Life

It was, my lung, most strange of you,
   A freak I cannot pardon,
Thus to transform yourself into
   A vegetable-garden.

Though laking William set erewhile
   His seal on rural fashions,
I must deplore, bewail, revile
   Your horticultural passions.

And as your ways I thus lament
   (Which, plainly, I call crazy)
For all I know, serene, content,
   You think yourself a daisy!

TRANSLATIONS
OF CHEROKEE INCANTATIONS

Love Charm

Ku! Listen! In Alahiya you repose, O Terrible Woman,
O you have drawn near to hearken.
There in Elayihi you rest, O White Woman.
When with you no one ever is lonely.
Most beautiful are you.
At once you have made me a white man.
When with me no one ever is lonely.
Now you you have made the path white for me.
Never shall it be dreary.
Now you have put me into it.
Never shall it become blue.
The white road you have brought down to me.
There in mid-earth you have placed me.
Upon the earth shall I stand erect.
When with me no one ever is lonely.
Into the white house you have led me.

There is Elayihi you have made the woman blue.
Now you have made the path blue for her.
Let her be wholly veiled in loneliness.
Where her feet are now and where ever she goes
Let loneliness leave its mark upon her.

Ha! I belong to the Wolf clan,
That one alone which was destined for you.
No one is ever lonely with me.
In the midst of men may she never think of them.
I belong to the one clan destined for you
When the seven clans were established.

For I was ordained to be a white man.
I stand with my face towards the sun.
No one is ever lonely with me.
Every where I am shadowed by the white house everlasting.

No one is ever lonely with me.
Your soul has come
Into the very core of my soul
Never to turn away.
I—I take your soul. Sge!

Charm to cure the bite of a snake.

Dunuwa, dunuwa, dunuwa, dunuwa, dunuwa, dunuwa.
Listen! Ha! It is only a common frog which
Has passed by and put it into you.

Dayuha, dayuha, dayuha, dayuha, dayuha, dayuha.
Listen! Ha! It is only an Usugi which
Has passed by and put it into you.

FROM A STUDY
OF ENGLISH METRICS

from
A STUDY OF ENGLISH METRICS

SYNOPSIS

That an important application of phonetics to metrical problems lies in the study of phonetic word-structure.

SUB-THESIS UNDER PRESENT CONSIDERATION

I. A type of vocabulary purely, or mainly, mono-dissyllabic, *i.e.*, showing a characteristic occurrence of polysyllables running from 0 to about 2%.

II. A type of medium structural complexity, *i.e.*, showing a characteristic occurrence of polysyllables running from about 3% to about 5 ½%, with a tendency to drop towards 2% and to rise towards 6%.

III. A type of extreme structural complexity, *i.e.*, showing a characteristic occurrence of polysyllables running from about 7% to about 8 ½%, with a tendency to drop towards 6% and to rise towards 9 ½% (or 10%?).

Note: The term "polysyllable" is used to include all words over two syllable as in length.

The discussion of the sub-thesis falls into three main parts:

A. Presentation of analysis
    1. Derivation of scale of polysyllabic occurrence for experimental testing from
        a. 125 Nursery Rhymes
        b. Milton (Table I)
        c. Pope (Table II)
    2. First testing of scale from the work of
        a. Tennyson (Table III)
        b. Swinburne (Table IV)
        c. Francis Thompson (Table V)
        d. Maurice Hewlett (Table VI)
B. Summary of three important points involved in differentiation of vocabularies
    1. Elementary word-forms entering into combination
    2. Range of values in word-accent
    3. Conditions of "weighting"
C. Importance of differentiation of vocabularies in study of Metrics indicated with reference to
    1. The problem as a whole
    2. Tennyson and the development of the decasyllable
    3. Swinburne and the development of triple rhymes

A STUDY OF ENGLISH METRICS

It is my object in the present discussion to venture the suggestion that an important application of phonetics to metrical problems lies in the study of phonetic word-structure. I have given first (in tentative formulation, of course) a specific conclusion with supporting data, and second a brief indication to the reasons for maintaining the general position. To deal with a definite, if still limited, range of fact before approaching the wider theoretical issues has seemed to me the better method, at least for the present. One offers thus as first evidence the results of systematic analysis and in so far as these possess, or seem to possess, a certain solidity and coherence within themselves, they are in some sort of a guarantee that the underlying theory is worthy of attention.

May I say that the statement here given is to be regarded as nothing more formal or definitive than a first rough summary drawn up in order to open discussion and (if the conclusions indicated will hold at all) to serve as a basis for correction and further investigation?

I.

The position taken can be outlined quickly and, for the time being, with I think fair explicitness in the following way. Scansion isolates, for the sake of analysis, the basic metrical units of verse—feet; the same analytical scrutiny must, I believe, be given to the basic phonetic units of speech—*i.e.*, phonetic word-forms—before we can possess sufficient data for the study of one of the fundamental problems of verse as a whole, the relation of the word to the foot. The scope of the proposed analysis must evidently parallel within its own field that of scansion within the metrical field; that is, as the study of English scansion deals with the whole possible variety of metrical units in English verse and with the special occurrence of these in individual poems, so the study of phonetic word-structure must deal with the whole variety of the word-forms existing in English and with the comparative occurrence of these in specific vocabularies.

Obviously there can be given, at this time, in support of the position outlined but a limited amount of experimental analysis, and as obviously, one must select for this first examination and presentation a group of facts which will yield results of main or central significance. Accordingly, I submit for immediate consideration, as summarizing what seems to be the most important single issue involved, the following tentative formulation, namely—

That the systematic analysis of English poems seems to indicate the existence of a tendency toward distinct structural differentiations of vocabulary, the main types being three in number:—

I. A type of vocabulary purely, or mainly, mono-dissyllabic.

II. A type showing medium structural complexity, *i.e.*, containing a medium number of words of three syllables and over.

III. A type showing extreme structural complexity, *i.e.*, containing an extreme number of words of three syllables and over.

Before proceeding to the discussion of this thesis, it is necessary to deal with certain questions of detail—more especially with certain difficulties—which are bound to arise in the actual carrying out of the work.

In the first place, even admitting it to be theoretically desirable, do we possess to-day a pronunciation sufficiently standardized to make possible the analysis of vocabularies on anything like the scale suggested? Variations in pronunciation are notorious. How can we be assured that a classification of the words in any given poem will represent the pronunciation of the poet who wrote? Is it not, rather, certain that the analysis will depend upon the pronunciation of the critic who dissects, and that the results of analysis will, consequently, vary with each new critic? And further, will not the difficulties be hopelessly increased when different historic periods are to be considered? No attempt is made to minimize these difficulties, nor, for the present, to meet them in detail. Two immediately practical considerations are, however, urged.

First, as to uncertainties of pronunciation *per se*. Nothing it should be noted is under present examination except syllabification (*i.e.*, the number of syllables); possible differences of accentuation do not enter into the matter at all. Moreover, since the classification of vocabularies in question is based on the relative occurrence of words of three syllables and over, only two groupings of words are dealt with: the mono-dissyllabic group regarded as a whole; the "polysyllabic" group regarded as a whole. As a practical matter of fact, therefore, as far as the present investigation is concerned, the cases of possible uncertainty narrow down to the particular group of words where there is a question between two and three syllables. I do not think that, however classified, the number of words in this group is large enough to affect, in any serious way, the general results obtained.

Second, as to the question of changing standards of pronunciation. Here again nothing is urged beyond the reduction to a minimum of the difficulties involved—in this case by selecting as far as possible work which allows the use of what may be roughly called the present standard of pronunciation. The single exception to this is the work of Milton. Here what may be roughly called the "Elizabethan" standard has been used. This statement, it is most hastily to be said, implies no absurd assertion that one has been able to reconstruct Elizabethan pronunciation as a whole. For the practical matter in hand, the main concern is simply with the fuller syllabification of a perfectly well-recognized class of words—the ion, ious, etc. class. In the analysis of Milton's vocabulary given below this fuller syllabification has been kept as consistently as possible—ocean, union, nation, for instance, being counted as trisyllables. It is to be noted, however, that the point made just previously holds here also. The results, as stated, would be affected only by the classification of those words where there is the question of a change from three to two syllables.

One somewhat smaller detail is still to be mentioned—the classification of compounds. The rule followed has been to regard compounds as whole words, many-fountained, for instance, being classed as a word of four syllables. In finer analysis it will, of course, become necessary to take into account the extent to which compounds are present in the whole polysyllabic group—as it is also necessary to take into account the extent to which proper nouns are present.

Turning now to my thesis, I have chosen the following poems for first analysis: (a) 125 Nursery Rhymes, (b) Paradise Lost and Samson Agonistes, (c) five of Pope's poems (see below). The reason for this selection is plain enough. If they exist at all, we have here, pretty clearly, examples of the three indicated types of vocabulary. It is difficult, at any rate, to imagine much doubt as to the facts that in Nursery Rhymes there are few "long" words, while Milton's is the great example in English verse of a polysyllabic vocabulary, or probably, as to the fact that Pope's vocabulary would come somewhere between these two extremes. The first business in hand is, therefore, to see whether systematic analysis will bear out this impression of differentiation where it is strongest, and, if so, what exacter arithmetical values are to be given to the words in which the range of difference has so far been expressed. What, in English, do we more precisely mean by "few" or "more," or "many" polysyllables?

My results for the 125 Nursery Rhymes are as follows: first, 59 of the Rhymes—very nearly half (47.2%)—are purely mono-dissyllabic; second, taking the Rhymes as a whole, of the total number of words used (6,928), 97.86% belong to the mono-dissyllabic group, 2.13% to the polysyllabic group.

At the lowest extreme may, therefore, be placed an occurrence of polysyllabic running from zero to about 2%.

The next section of analysis—that of Milton and Pope—can best be given in tabulated form. (See p. 21.)

Summarizing: the tables show a characteristic occurrence of polysyllables in Milton's poems running from about 7% to about 8 ½%, with a tendency to drop toward 6% and rise to 9%, and a characteristic occurrence in the poems by Pope running from about 4% to about 5 ½%.

These figures may be held, tentatively, to represent the extreme and medium occurrence of polysyllabes.

Restating now the description of the types as at first given here we have:

I. A type of vocabulary purely, or mainly, mono-dissyllabic: *i.e.*, containing a characteristic occurrence of words of three syllables and over, running from 0 to about 2%.

TABLE I.

MILTON	Total No. of words	Per cent Mono-disyllabic	Per cent Polysyllabic
Paradise Lost I......	5,960	91.67	8.33
II......	7,917	92.24	7.75
III......	5,566	92.07	7.92
IV......	7,700	92.74	7.24
V......	6,804	92.01	7.99
VI......	6,773	90.95	9.03
VII......	4,774	91.40	8.58
VIII......	4,921	91.45	8.53
IX......	9,010	93.01	6.98
X......	8,370	91.74	8.24
XI......	6,859	92.48	7.50
XII......	4,930	91.78	8.21
Total.............	79,584	92.03	7.95
Samson Agonistes			
Dialogue.............	9,465	92.04	7.94
Choruses.............	3,427	90.92	9.08
Total.............	12,892	91.75	8.23

TABLE II.

POPE	Total No. of words	Per cent Mono-disyllabic	Per cent Polysyllabic
Essay on Criticism......	5,744	94.91	5.08
The Rape of the Lock...	6,149	94.71	5.28
Elegy—Unfortunate Lady	652	95.86	4.14
Essay on Man I......	2,288	94.32	5.68
II......	2,251	94.32	5.68
III......	2,481	94.43	5.56
IV......	3,141	95.54	4.46
Total.............	10,161	94.72	5.27
Epistle to Dr. Arbuthnot	3,353	95.91	4.09

TABLE III.

TENNYSON	Total No. of words	Per cent Mono- disyllabic	Per cent Polysyllabic
Oenone................	1,988	94.31	5.68
Ulysses..............:..	556	96.94	3.05
Tithonus..............	599	96.33	3.67
The Coming of Arthur...	4,256	96.54	3.45
Merlin and Vivien......	7,896	95.88	4.10
Lancelot and Elaine.....	11,799	95.83	4.15
The Holy Grail.........	7,474	96.48	3.50
Guinevere..............	5,671	95.68	4.30
The Passing of Arthur...	3,855	96.59	3.39

TABLE IV.

SWINBURNE	Total No. of words	Per cent Mono- disyllabic	Per cent Polysyllabic
Chastelard I....:.....	4,712	98.59	1.40
II..........	3,975	98.56	1.43
III..........	3,703	98.65	1.35
IV..........	7,061	98.30	1.68
V..........	6,001	98.18	1.81
Total..............	25,452	98.42	1.57
Atalanta in Calydon			
Dialogue.............	12,832	95.84	4.14
Choruses.............	5,536	96.83	3.17
Total..............	18,368	96.14	3.85
Hymn to Proserpine.....	1,003	97.50	2.49
Hesperia..............	1,283	97.03	2.96
The Forsaken Garden...	671	98.80	1.19

II. A type of medium structural complexity: *i.e.*, containing a characteristic occurrence of words of three syllables and over, running from about 4% to about 5 ½%, with, probably, a tendency to drop towards 3% and to rise toward 6%.

III. A type of extreme structural complexity: *i.e.*, showing a characteristic occurrence of words of three syllables and over, running from about 7% to about 8 ½%, with a tendency to drop towards 6% and to rise 9%.

The next step is to see how far the scheme thus roughly established can be applied with reference to the vocabularies of other poems. Here selection has been made—always the selection of *whole* poems—from the work of Tennyson, Swinburne, Francis Thompson and Mr. Maurice Hewlett. The results of analysis are given in tabulated form.

It is clear that these vocabularies fall readily into the suggested classification.

In the work of Tennyson the vocabulary used is of the "medium" type, but it is to be remarked that while the poems of Pope under analysis the tendency is to rise from 4% toward 5%, there is here a tendency to drop from 4% toward 3%.

Also of the medium type, "Atlanta in Calyndon" shows the same tendency, while the "Hymn to Proserpine" and "Hesperia" drop still further, from 3% towards 2%. In "Chastelard" and "The Forsaken Garden" the occurrence, under 2% is that of the first type. The use of so markedly mono-dissyllabic a vocabulary is, of course, particularly to be noted in a poem of the length of "Chastelard."

The work of Francis Thompson, without any analysis easily to be recognized as of the "extreme" polysyllabic type, shows, under analysis, in the three poems chosen, the characteristic occurrence derived from Milton—7% to 9%.

Mr. Maurice Hewlett, on the other hand, uses in his trilogy, "The Agonists," the medium type of vocabulary, with, as in the case of Tennyson, the 3-4% occurrence rather than the 4-5% exemplified by Pope.

Thus the only changes to be made as the result of this section of analysis are to give 2% as the lower limit of polysyllabic occurrence for the medium type of vocabulary and to indicate a slight tendency to rise above 9% in the extreme type, taking 9 ½% (or, perhaps, even 10%?) as the experimental upper limit.

TABLE V.

FRANCIS THOMPSON	Total No. of words	Per cent Mono- disyllabic	Per cent Polysyllabic
The Hound of Heaven...	1,205	92.61	7.38
An Anthem of Earth....	2,798	90.59	9.39
Sister Songs I...........	2,658	92.02	7.97
II........	5,457	92.11	7.89
Total...............	8,115	92.06	7.92

TABLE VI.

MAURICE HEWLETT	Total No. of words	Per cent Mono- disyllabic	Per cent Polysyllabic
Minos, King of Crete....	7,882	96.41	3.59
Ariadne in Naxos.......	8,325	95.92	4.07
Death of Hippolytus....	8,080	95.96	4.03

SELECTED LETTERS

Adelaide T. Crapsey
[1893]
Kemper Hall, Kenosha, Wisconsin
6 fols.

My dearest Mamma

At last we know when vacation begins. We leave here on the 21st of Dec and come back the 6th of January. That is I reach home one week from next Sunday. I have to travel on Sunday both coming and going but I guess I can stand that. Does it seem possible that the vacation is so nearly here? Emily is going to write you today about Mays invitation. As there are not going to be any other girls here this Xmas I think it would be nice for her to go and of course it would not be any more expensive which is the chief thing to consider. She has not said anything about [it] to me lately so I don't know what she thinks about it.

Mr Burton Holmes lectured here the other night on Spain. He is becoming [undeciphered word ends in "ly"] monotonous. He started to show us pictures of the bullfights but Sister wouldn't let him. Said it was not "proper." Mary Draper is back. I went over to her on Thursday which is the reason why I did not write. We have a lecture on Art this week and an Exhibition in gyms. Next week are Exams. How I hate them. But we never think much of Exams when a holliday comes right after them. In the way of work everything is the same as usual. I've got two themes to write and not an idea what to write about which is a delightful situation. I wrote one about Algy the other day which Miss Ramsey [?] said was "very good indeed". French is out of sight. I enjoy it more than anything else. There are only two of us in the class you know and we are simply flying. We are reading "The Black July", one of Dumas you know, now. I expect to finish that some time this week and start another one. You must have had a fine time thanksgiving with all the cream at home. I am so sorry Phil is not getting on at Catskill. I wish he could go somewhere where there is more life.

Did you get the Kodacs [the Kemper Hall *Kodak*, the school newspaper]—What did you think of Emilys "told by the Roadside." Wasn't it out of sight? Miss Adams rarely raved over it and a thing has to be pretty good for that. We are beginning now to work over the December number. Thank fortune I have not the editorials to write this year but it will be turn next. Our class gave a sleigh ride last Tuesday night. We had a fine time.

Has Rachel seen about my "Diana of the Crossways". Tell her she will be an angel if she will.

I suppose it is about time to talk about the money for my ticket. Papa knows how much that is doesn't he? O dear! I feel as if it were awfully selfish to take all that money for traveling expensis. If you think I had better I will stay here this vacation too. Doesn't Papa know some railroad man he can get a pass from?

Love to all + especiall[y] you + P.A.
Ever affectioeatly
Adelaide

Adelaide T. Crapsey
[1893]
Kemper Hall, Kenosha, Wisconsin
5 fols.

My dearest Mamma

Emily and I were no end glad to get your letter today. I am so glad you have had your picture taken but I'm sorry they did not turn out better. When will we get them. Soon I hope for we are awfully anxious to see them. Harrys pictures are very good don't you think.

I am glad you like the pictures I sent, every one here does too. It is very good of all of us that is as good as a group can be. They are the girls I go with most and like the best. The first girl (Grace Chapman) + the third Louisa Cary (beginning with the tallest) I like about as well as any girls in school. They are mighty nice. The sixth one is my roommate Ada Ferry [?]. Don't you think she looks awfully nice and jolly. She is I can tell you and we get on beautifully. We say with pride that we haven't had even the beginning of a scrap since we roomed together. We have already decided to room together next year and are going to ask for Emily's room.

Charlie sent me a dear box of Huylers the other day and a letter. I must write + thank him. Its too bad isn't it that he is not in Rochester. He seems to think there is no hope of his going their [there] again either. Got a letter from Hawley yesterday which was of course foot-ball from beginning to end. They are jubilant at Princeton + are going to do Yale up if it takes a neck.

I am so glad you have a cook and if she only will turn out as well as Annie did wont it be smooth—And you've engaged a nurse for Charly allready! If Charily isn't a boy I wont speak to her. Emily has only mentioned her "plan" to me once—you know I see very little of her—and then she seemed to think it would be the best thing to do. I cant bear either to think of you all alone when you are ill and wish we could both be there—but if only one of us can

I suppose Emily would be lots more help than I. You know by sad experience that I'm pretty much of a good for nothing. However we needn't decide yet.

Love to everybody and lots for yourself "Adelaide" dear

lovingly
Adelaide

Adelaide T. Crapsey
1908
En route to Europe
1 fol. [letterhead "Hamburg-Amerika Linie/Genua-Via Roma, 4/
Telegramm-Addresse Hapag, Genua"]

Dear Mother—

Gibraltar is nearly here and the rain is pouring down. The coast of Africa is supposed to be in sight but because of the fog it isn't. We've had a fair voyage. No storms but a tremendous swell that has sent the ship from side to side with tiresome regularity. It hasn't been cold at all.

I'm not going to try to write much—Its so hot + stuffy inside— and ones mind doesn't work on shipboard—or mine doesnt.

How I wonder how you all are. Is this going to reach you any where around Christmas? Dont work too hard and have Elizabeth to help out. Everything has been very nice—one voyage is very like another.

Now I'm going to rush out on deck. This is almost the first time I've been here (in the writing room) since we started. Its over the dining room and smells abound.

Heaps of love to you all, I'll send another line from Napels— and really write when we get to Rome.

A merry Christmas + a happy New Year—to you and the children + Mr Seward

Lovingly—Adelaide

Adelaide T. Crapsey
1909
Rome
6 fols.

Dear Mamma: I have been searching Paris editions of the Herald and the Daily Mail for more news from Rochester but there is nothing to be found. That means I hope that the fires—two of them at once, one paper said—were not too dreadful—at any rate in loss of life. One fire, a telegram in the Herald reported, was in one of the foreign sections—down by the station I seemed to make out. If that is so the Brotherhood must be doing heaps of relief work. There must be still another week or ten days before I can hear directly. I am waiting so anxiously for word.

If I were sure that it wouldn't come in upon a very sad time with you all I could be writing a most lighthearted letter. The weather has been so lovely. Italy is really at times everything that people say it is; enchanting skies, flowers all coming out and everything fresh and clean and beautiful. As for me I'm feeling better than I have for three straight years and its perfectly joyous. I am so sorry that that over a month ago letter of mine worried you. I tried hard not to have it sound worrisome.

The Merrits left yesterday and of course I shall miss them—but wasn't is nice that they were here really so long—a whole month. Oh I must tell you a funny thing. One day Louise wanted to go out to the Protestant Cemetary to see Keat's grave. You know I'm not much of a person for doing things like that and I never had been there. When we got out there we went, by mistake, into the new section and after hunting in vain for the grave we went back to the gate and I was just asking the woman who seemed to be in charge of things, where to go when an American came in—a rather lost looking man (I mean he seemed not to know his way) with a bunch of carnations and while I was talking to the woman I heard him ask Louise if this were the Protestant Cemetary and how could he find the grave of James Lee. Louise offered him my small amount of Italian so when I had finished about Keats he told me over again what he wanted, and I told the portiere and she showed him the book where all the registrations are; and of course all the time I was hunting in my mind for James Lee because the name was perfectly familiar and then I remembered about Professor Lee so I said to the unknown American—"Is it Professor Lee's grave?" and of course he said yes and then in a brief conversation it came out that I knew the Lees, that I had known them not in Milton [?] but in Rochester—the unknown American had known them at Canadagua [Canandaigua]—why so had I; we had had a cottage there—so had he—our cottage was Vine Cottage and (in a sudden burst of information) my name was Crapsey—Oh! then he knew who I was, and I knew who he was—his name was—Sherman Morse.

Wasn't that odd? Do you remember how we used to watch all the grown up people at the "Stone House"—but of course in all the ten summers we were there I never spoke to Sherman Morse. He was much too grown up, just engaged do you remember. And now after some sixteen years I meet him, in a place where I've never been before and where I'll probably never go again—and on one of the two days that he had in Rome. He had come over with Roosevelt and was returning at once.

A young man across the way is tying his tie with as much thought as I spend over a whole getting dressed from the ground up. His mirror is hung square in the middle of the window and of course he is perfectly visible to every one in this house. It takes him a solid three quarters of an hour to part his hair.

My awnings have just been put up and they will be a great help as it gets warmer. I saw Dr Gauigan yesterday and he said he thought I might perfectly well stay through June—he and I both being of the opinion that its safer to stay where I am than to use up energy packing and traveling and getting used to a new place. Really I'm afraid to budge for fear I'll disturb this present heavenly state of things.

Oh, what do you think of me with a dentist! Now I know what

a rubber dam is. Really I was awfully thankful to get the things done. One tooth had been bothering me ever since I left home but I didn't quite dare begin until your hundred came and then I thought that was the best first thing to do with it. As a matter of fact I should have been driven to it anyhow as the place was getting worse every day—the nerve was exposed and had to be killed.

I wonder how you all are and what you are doing. Your garden must be starting now, the flowers I mean. Tell Marie I'm really going to write to her. Love to you all and to Mr Seward—and everyone. Remember me to Inez—How does all the domestic machinery go?

Lovingly—Adelaide.

Adelaide T. Crapsey, Algernon S. Crapsey, et. al.
1909
Hotel does Etats Unis, Paris
5 fols. [4 fols. holograph]

Remember you only need a 2 cent stamp.
c/o—The American Express Co.
5 — 6 Haymarket
London—England—
(I don't know the Herne Bay address yet—will send it later)

Dear Mother and Father—and all the family. Here I am safe and sound in Paris. We changed our plans at Genoa—took a train on Saturday night instead of Sunday morning and got here on Sunday afternoon at two oclock. The night journey was what night journeys always are. The train was crowded, everybody packed on top of everyone else. We did not get a whole compartment—nor even all in one. We alternated between suffocating tunnels and icy alps. Sleep of course was out of the question. We kept up our spirits with Marsalla (a very special kind of Italian wine) and weakened coffee at four o'clock in the morning—and some more at six. So you see we lived through it—and even found it amusing in some spots. But oh, such dirt and dust! I've really come through most awfully well. Poor Mary Draper caught cold on the Alps and has been laid up almost ever since.

We are staying in a funny little Latin Quarter hotel—L'Hotel des Etats Unis—(Hotel of the United States)—I have my room and breakfast and dinner for 5.50-the extra 50 because I have a room alone—the others are in double rooms and get off with five. We lunch out in various small restaurants—a franc is the limit—so I'm living on 6.50 a day. I had hoped for 5–but thats not to be done short of doing ones own housekeeping. Well I'm going down anyhow and when I get to England it will be less than 5.

The place is a[s] clean as can be—and that let me tell you is a rarer thing on this side than on that. There are plain painted pine floors—just little rugs, no carpets, iron beds, good simple furniture, and very good meals. Its really a nice little place.

Mrs Thomas writes that she will be in the cottage and ready for me on the 6th—so I think I shall go straight there and not to London at all. She says the cottage is ever so nice and the air splendid. Fraulein Romer has sent on my trunk from Rome—-so I'll be all settled very soon.

As usual I'm not trying to do any sightseeing. We are near the Luxembourg Gardens and I've been there—and to the Museum—also to the Pantheon. Next week I'm going to get over to the Louvre.

How are you all? I expect I'll be hearing in a little while. The winter work is beginning and you [will] all be as busy as ever.

The inevitable finances appear on the next page—also I enclose Mrs Draper's account with me up to date. For once you'll have a businesslike statement of my expenses. Isn't it nice of her to do it?—and she's looking after everything here too. I thought it might amuse Mr Seward to see it. Tell him its all his present. Oh, and I enclose too a quaint little letter from Fraü'lein Römer—I thought it might amuse you to see it too.

Love to you all—Adelaide

Cash on hand—	500 francs
Journey up—	133.35
Hotel + lunch—3 weeks—	136.50
Journey to England—	50.00

500.00
319.85
180.15 = $36.50. Out of whole must come laundry—tips— the express charges on my trunk from Rome—the general odds and ends of expenses like stamps and hairpins—the little extra emergency money that its safer to have—and my "seeing Paris" expenses—which I will make mild—almost nonexistent. But I'm awfully afraid I won't have much between me and the world when

I go to Herne Bay. Yet I've tried to be as careful as possible and its made it ever so much cheaper traveling in a group. If I could have $50 it would take me along for a little while. It seems too perfectly horrid to be consuming the family resources to this extent.

[fol. 5 in Mrs Draper's hand]	
Adelaide Crapsey To Credit	307.70
Ticket to Paris	87.35
Luggage from San G. to Florence	2.00
Lunch to Genoa - - - -	1.95
Fees at Florence station-	2.75
Excess luggage - - - -	4.20
Fees + omnibus arriving G.	1.15
" " " leaving G.	1.90
Hotel bill + extra dinner	12.45
Bath	2.00
Hotel fees at Genoa - -	3.60
Lunch for Paris train—	1.25
Dinner on train - -	4.50
Pillow - - - -	.60
Porters, Cab + luggage Paris	2.60
Paris telegram - - - - - - -	60
Cafe at lait - - - -	1.20
Tulle	
Lunch Monday Paris	
Drive in Genoa	95
	130.25

Cr. 307.70
   130.25
   177.45 Due A. Crapsey

     1.35
      .80
     2.15

Algernon S. Crapsey and Adelaide T. Crapsey
24 May 1910
London
10 fols.

May 24. The reason for this proud date is that I am at the British Museum and they make you date your book slips—so that I do know for once what the date is.

Dear Father and Mother—

I was ever so glad to have the letter from home last night. When I hear I am always afraid that something is going wrong and you aren't telling me about it. You must have been having great times with politics and united Charities. Hurray for Mother on a platform! And thank you very much for the check. Maybe your daughter will manage to get on her own feet again sometime—and her hopes at the present are brighter than usual and for these reasons.

You remember I said that I hoped to get my work in order by the end of May—enough I mean so that I could tell whether it amounted to anything. Well I have been working just as hard as I could and I have got at any rate this far—I have sent to an English Prosodist—a Mr. T.S. Omond—an account of an experiment I have been trying and this very morning came a letter from him from which I will copy the parts that will show you what in general he thinks. I would send the letter but it has a lot of technical discussion in it that I must keep to answer. I ought to say that I wrote first to ask him if I might—and he said yes—politely but not enthusiastically. Of course it took heaps of courage but I couldn't think of anything else to do. [A leaf seems to be missing from Adelaide Crapsey's letter.] " . . . your paper when completed and have no doubt it would be gladly accepted (No pay I fear but prosodists must not look for pecuniary reward!)

I feel sure that it is only on lines like yours that progress can be made."

Then the rest is about technical points—three large pages—with to end up with the hope that I will write again soon, that he will be happy be of use in any way—and that he is obliged to me for letting him see my work.

And I dont pretend to be anything but tremendiously pleased and tremendiously relieved at such a judgement from a man who has been working at the subject for some thirty years or so and who has read practically everything that has been written on it. To tell you the truth I can hardly believe my eyes. I was quite ready to have him cool—or crushing—and I wasn't going to be hopelessly discour[a]ged even by that. As you know I have worked alone and in an interrupted scrappy way. I might have made all sorts of mistakes—or the whole way of working might have seemed wrong. But you see it has turned out well and I am glad that I finally screwed up my courage to do it—to send him the work I mean. Of course this is by no means the end of my difficulties. But it is the assurance that I have got a useable amount of material. The idea of publishing is most surprising to me. I hadn't dreamed the thing was worked out enough for that—(The M.S. in question by the way is only of these pages in length)—Me in the Modern Language Review is a little funny isn't it? And I am not sure that I want to unless it would be the only means toward getting a job. If I can get a job that will let me go on working a bit longer I would like it better. You see I have so far gone just as carefully as I could and I want to keep on that way. However we'll see. I will be writing again to Mr Omond and I will let you know everything as soon as I know it.

So you see—I am able to say that I think the work amounts to something and that I can go on with it—and this prosodist will make it pay—or at least if I can't then I will give it up. Both of you have been perfectly splendid through all this time—and I never can tell you how grateful I am. If I do come out anywhere it will be because you have been so patient over this hard time. It makes me wriggle every time I think of just the money burden of it to you.

Please excuse this scrawly letter—but I wanted to let you know right away. I've said this is private because it really doesnt represent anything definite to talk about outside of ones own family. And the letter is just a private letter that I would only quote in this way to you. Also any talk about publishing still seems to me too vague—and too absurd!—to talk about. So this letter is just for you two and the older ones—the Duchess and Paul—if you think it will interest them It isn't that I am secretive but that one hates to talk much about work in the experimental stage—so all this is strictly for the family.

By the way don't be disturbed if you don't know much what Prosody is. Hardly anyone does.

This is a disjointed scrawl. To tell the truth I've been working very hard and I'm pretty tired. This silly health of mine is most inconvenient.

Please forgive me for not telling all about the funeral and Kings and things. How I wished that I could have changed places with Arthur for that week. The crowds and crepe and long waitings that kept me from seeing much wouldn't have bothered him and he would have had a glorious time—even if it was a funeral.

I do hope you are all well—and that all the work is going on as splendidly as usual. As I know more of my own plans I will let you know. Thank you again for the money and everything

Your loving and grateful daughter

Adelaide.

My best love to Duchess + the Babies if they are there and to all the family and Mr Seward. As soon as I have any definite plans I will write and tell him about it if you think he would find it interesting?

As I read this over I seem to be giving an exaggerated importance to a not very important thing—but you see this is the first time I've had anything but my own judgement to go by and I really cant help feeling encouraged.

This is a Private letter to you and Father

Adelaide T. Crapsey and Algernon S. Crapsey
23 February 1911
Plainfield, New Jersey
3 fols.

Thursday—
Feb—23d

Dearest Mother and Father—

Did you ever know such funny luck! Of course its a great chance
to get work at Smith and I felt that it would be flying in the face of
providence to refuse but Oh dear me! why did it come just when I
want to see you all. Well the spring vacation will be here soon—and
the summer one. Thats a comfort. A telegram this morning says to
go to Northampton as soon as possible but I'll take the time for a
flying trip home whether or no. I'll leave here tonight—(will wire
train later)—have Friday + Saturday + perhaps Sunday at home.
Can Father wait and go to New York on Saturday? Then I can see
him on Friday. The whole thing wont be much but it will be better
than nothing wont it? Oh dear! Isnt it all funny. Its what comes of
being born a Crapsey!
     I would like awfully to go to Cornell to see Professor Sampson.
Do you suppose it could be managed on Sunday? Then I would go
straight from Ithaca to Northampton. Will Father look up trains?—
Of course if it can't be managed I can write. My Prosody work and
the Fellowship at Cornell is the main thing of course but the work
at Smith will give me some money now and whats more a very
good connection with things academica. After my three years—or
nearly—disconnection that is the main thing + really great luck.
     Arthur is waiting for this letter and I want it to go at once.
     Well—I'll see you all tomorrow morning. I am so dreadfully
dreadfully sorry Mother dear to upset things so. And after all the
waiting for that slow old steamer! But we must take what the Gods
send I suppose.

Love to you all. Can you arrange so that I can see Mrs Watson + Mrs Willard.

And wont I be glad to see you—and *isnt* it funny.

Lovingly, Adelaide.

Today Rachel + I are re-packing and putting clothes in order. Will wire train later.

Jean Webster
19 September 1914
Rochester, New York
2 fols.

Dear Jean— I'm just most awfully glad about the play. The press is certanly "good"—and Ziegfield who came here on Tuesday told Mr Corris the play was "a complete success" "a perfect knockout"—and if that isn't the voice of the box office I dont know what is. So now your off!—and I hope your not dead to celebrate—

If this is unusually inane forgive it. Present breakdown worst of lot— I'm back in bed with a trained nurse and every bit of strength I ever had vanished— Isn't it sort of tiresome. I enclose Dr Baldwin's letter— I've written Dr Hance + will let you know what he says— Paul has been to Brown's Mills + reports the country + air as everything one could wish—"a piece of southern Georgia picked up and put down in between N.Y. + Phila." The Sanatorium was closed (it's a winter place it seems) but Paul says its a nice enough little establishment to look at + in a most lovely grove of pine and oak. It remains to see what the medical opinion of it is. I do hope + pray it will be all right It seems to me I just must get settled

Horrid of me to come down in the middle of your success with all my everlasting troubles—Wasnt it all awful the last days + rather fun too especially at the end—a regular grand Broadway first night! I wish I'd been there to see you clutch the "floral tributes"—and all the rest. I wonder whether I'll ever see that play! I suppose you'll tinker for a week or two— I hope not more—Really aren't you all feeling, alowing for natural qualms + such, as if the thing were launched.

Paul says theres a dear little hotel at Browns Mills with delicious cooking— It might be just the place for you to vanish to (when you can) for a few days rest.

Its funny how weak I am— I've never been so weak. Dear me troubles again!

Remember me to everyone—tell me how the play goes—the details I mean

Adelaide

Isnt Dr Baldwin ever so nice about it all—

17 July 1913
Hillcrest Hospital, Pittsfield, Massachusetts
3 fols. 5 pp.

Hillcrest Hospital
Pittsfield— Mass
July 17—1913

Dear E— What do you think of that? But as you see I can still hold a pen! How are you and where are you and what have you been doing? I do hope it has been and is being awfully nice and restful—

Here's telegraphic report of my news. I finished the favorite literature and sent it off on Saturday the 21st of June. I reckoned that it would take P.E.M [Paul Elmer More, editor of *The Nation*] about 3 weeks to get around to reading his surprise and settled back to rest during that time. It came back on Tuesday the 23d of June— but with (not to employ the method of suspense) a really very nice (if in spots funny) letter. The thing was too long for the Nation but I seem to have "hit on a very interesting point"—but the argument was hard to follow (E! that masterpiece of lucidity!) and " 'it would be a satisfaction to me personally if I could see your argument shorn of all secondary issues and presented in its barest skeleton." Being willing to oblige I sat me down—(after a day or two to get my breath) and ripped the favorite literature up the back and did a condensed version—sending it off to be typed on the 7th of July— I stayed in Tyringham to avoid the interrupting packing + unpacking. Of course in the meanwhile I had written Mr More saying that I would like very much to send the shorter paper—and getting in reply a nice little note with his vacation address—to send the thing to. On the 8th of July as I got out of my bath I leaned over quickly felt a remarkable pain and after a second found it more discrete to drop full length on the bathroom floor than to stand up. After a while I got up grabbed a nightdress—and retired again to the floor. No not really fainting—just staving it off by lying flat you know. It was awfully funny. After one moment or two I got back to my room and went to bed and we got—or rather the others got hot water bags + such and it really was a[w]fully funny—and nothing at all serious— Just one of those things you can do by a queer little twist—the filament of a muscel or something broke. But of course we didnt know that + decided not to take chances so in we motored to a doctor— He has turned out to be a very nice sensible person—poked about settled the back as nothing—it was better by that time anyhow—but told me the best thing I could do would be to cut hospital for three or four week—-have some mild treatment, absolute rest etc—and here I am. As a matter of fact I think its been rather a lucky chance. I'm rather tireder than I thought I was and I'm positively thankful to be here.

The new version of the F.L. [Favorite Literature] is back and ready to go as soon as I can look it over. This is my off time so I'm waiting a little. I shall get it off by about the 21st which isnt bad. As a matter of fact I knew that I ought to have a condensed thing like that but I hadn't had time or energy to tackle it— I'm very glad to have done it. There are only 16 pages including synopsis and notes— It doesnt include the whole argument—keeps just to the point of the vocabularies—but I think maybe the others too complicated (for anyone but us!) without a simpler first statement.

Forgive this scribble— I'll be here four weeks anyhow— Isnt it funny— I'm hoping to hear from you and I'll be furious with fate if you havent had a truly nice time— How has the weather been—

No more at peril! Your—A.C.

By the way this is all just for you— about P.E.M + the paper and all that.

As for the Hospital I'm not going out of my way to keep it a secret— but I'm not going out of my way to publish it in Northampton—would you?

Miss Esther Lowenthal/c/o The American Express Co/Paris—France [readdressed: Madame Gaulier/72 rue de Seine/ Paris] Pittsfield, Mass./9 PM/ Jul 17/1913

2 October 1913
Saranac Lake, N.Y.
1 fol. 2 pp.

Thursday Oct 2

Esther! Punch! You've been wicked again— But I forgot all protests in sheer joy at the sight of the nice old cover and in a gay morning pouring over the innards— I took it, you see, slowly and with discrimination—"savoured" it as Arnold Bennett says (I hate the word)— Its a particularly nice number (Sept 17th) especially as to the delectable newspaper quotations— I call your attention especially to the five pups (p 240) and Mrs Coverdale Bentnick (p 243) I am also your debtor to the extent of several time-beguiling notes and the writing paper. By some queer freak or other I had just remembered that that was in my desk and meant to tell you to use it your self. But it will come in handy—thank you for sending it. You know how heroic it seems to me to "do up" packages—

To think that one had lived to regret faculty meetings. I fairly wept to think of what I had missed—"filthy cabal" and "brutal frankness"— What language wont be flying about before that curriculum gets reformed. Isnt Mrs Eastman too amazing— Mr Bassets comment on the handsome barkeep is a double delight— as being perfect in itself and as coming from Mr Basset—whod'a thought it.

If you and Mary think it perfectly fair to let my application for leave stand of course I'll do it and feel rather relieved—less swing off into space without any connection anywhere. Of course no one knows what the Trustees will say—but we can leave that to them as you say. My mind is beginning to come alive again and I have hopes that I can do some work on the favorite Literature after say another month or two. You know there is still the Carnegie thing to try—in Washington I mean.

Dr. Baldwin is very nice indeed, very quiet—and very cautious.

Its a great relief to me to find that he is as careful about his greys as I am. Grey overcoat, grey other things, grey tie and a scarf pin of some cloudy grey crystal— All of this I am sure will be a great help. (These frivolous comments for your ear alone)— I seem to be going on very well—whether its fundamental or not I'll tell you when I know. I'm still on this silly "absolute quiet" regime— I'll be glad when I can at least brush my own hair and take my own bath.

Remember me to the Lady of the House + C.B. and Mary and every one— Some time when you are in the library + think of it tell Miss Tyler it was ever so nice to get her letter—(item—she says Mr Schutz says he's to have 1300 new books)— No more at present in deference to orders—though I really feel perfectly well— Are you keeping up with milk eggs steak at Boydens and all the other things you must do— Really how are you feeling— any less tired than last year or just the same? Yours Adelaide and thank you for everything. [Written in left margin parallel to side of page: 'Lest this seem an unnatural letter I add a request— some time—*any* time will do—if its not packed away will you send me the volume of my Chaucer that has Troilus and Cressida (not sure of the spelling) in it—(There are 2 Chaucers one in one volume with horrid fine print and one in 3 vols—)]

Miss Esther Lowenthal/10 West Street/ Northampton—Mass. Saranac Lake, N.Y./I PM/ Oct 2/1913

24-25 November 1913
Saranac Lake, N.Y.
6 fols. 6 pp.

Dear E— Such accumulations of things— The Japanese pictures—the Atlantic—the Poetry Review—the catalogues—and the letters— Oh, dont stop sending news—until you grow weary. I was frightfully sorry (to take the last letter first) to hear about Maude— I expected something of the sort—but not quite so soon— Do you hear anything else—more definite?

Did you get the wretched little scrawl I sent you last—one all unworthy of its occassion? My bank account is the blither for your crime— I can only repeat you ought not to and you ought not to! My news—to be as usual egotistic—is as I wrote you most encouraging. Dr Baldwin was really this time (last examination—the day I wrote you) quite different—instead of being non-commuttal [noncommittal] (spelling?) and cautious he was quite openly optimistic. He feels that the throat complication is pretty well in hand—inflamation gone and little sign or danger of tubercular infection. The lungs havent begun to heal yet but they are no worse which is a sign that the disease is loosing its activity—the famous "arresting" processe. I dont know why I trouble you with these gruesom details—the sum total is that I think he (Dr Baldwin) feels now that the thing's going to be manageable— Of course just how strong I'll ever manage to be—and whether I can get back to a teaching job and if so when—these are all on the knees of the Gods. My fatigue (technical term "prostration") is ever with me—but that I can manage—

I'm writing this sitting up in bed on an out of door porch with heavy woolen gloves on— Can you read a word of it— The "out of-door" treatment means for me—now—from 10 to 4 or 5 or so on an out of door porch—or, if I dont get up from 10 to about 2.30   Then for the last day or two I've dressed and gone out again—another porch—or, blessed relief, a drive—I've had 3 of these for 3 days in succession and thank Heaven for them. After the eternal no movement its the greatest relief. Dr Baldwin says to try things—but of course very slowly, + very gently—which I religiously do. Jean Webster is up here for a few days—got here Saturday morning. Its awfully nice to have some one around— Does it still linger in your mind that you might come for a bit in the holydays or between semesters? Horrid of me even to suggest a long journey to a cold place! I'm going to try to stick it out up here unless it gets too impossible, I think Dr Baldwin is awfully good and as I've never had any consecutive medical care I think it would be a good thing to try it. Also the cold is really better if one can stand it. Ive got to decide what to do next—whether to stay here—or where to go—this house I mean—I'm glad Jean is up here during the process—

The fav. lit. [favorite literature] hangs fire— I was laid up a week after Dr Baldwin told me I might work—and in the 3 or 4 days since then Ive spent most of my extra energy in dressing and driving.

Interruption—letter from Claude Bragdon and book— Wait till I've opened them— another Man the Cube?

Next door to it *A Primer of Higher Space*—"hot from the press"—but I'm horrid even to smile—he really is so awfully nice. Did I tell you that he (Mr Bragdon—my pronouns are awful this morning—well my hands are cold!)—that he and Mr Tucker wrote me letters that you could just have interchanged—only one used Xian [Christian] Science terms + the other Indian Philosophy— Both awfully sweet nice letters—but it was a little funny wasn't it—

I do hope (to return) that I can get at the metrical stuff in ernest soon—even to the extent of tackling the 2d paper after I get this one off to the Modern Language Review— But of course I'll be guided—well mainly by my pulse, I suppose— How silly! The Poetry Review like the others—thin and stodgy but a degree more provincial more amateurish—(whats happening to intellectual life in England!) Not much good for fav. Lit I fear— You'll notice the delightful implication that my intellectual life is neither thin, stodgy, provincial nor amateurish!

Next day

This letter only half finished but I'll send it and continue in my next— as to confidences of my chief—Poet Noyes—etcetc—your note of Sunday Evening is meanwhile here—glad you are going to hear Padervisky [Paderewski]—and with C.B.! Dear me! Do tell me about Poet Noyes and Keats.

The cold weather complicates matters— I stay out of doors but so bundled up—(and it will get worse) that any activity esp. such a one as writing is next to impossible— What a bore—

The Japanese pictures are awfully nice—how did you think of them?—and everything else— more later— *Can* you read this?— Usual messages to every one—and official information that I'm much better— Tell Mary especially—

I *am* so sorry about Maud Temple— Let me know what you hear— How are you yourself— *Dont* join the disabled lot—

More later (though enough here heaven knows) Adelaide—

Man the Cube bound in with Primer of Higher Space— my 3d copy!

Miss Esther Lowenthal/ 10 West Street / Northampton / Mass. aranac Lake, N.Y./6 PM/ Nov 25/1913

24 March 1914
Saranac Lake, N.Y.
4 fols. 4 pp.

Dear E.— I can only suggest that M. Schintz was so convinced of
the incompetence of his department that he felt it perfectly safe to say
anything—in French. If you do manage to lay hands on the famous
(or infamous) thing do send it—I'll return it. I'm sure it will be worth
saving. But really of all the impossible things I think this the most
impossible—It cant be possible (can it?) that Mr Burton knew about
it—ahead I mean. What further news of the departure of the bar-
keep? Mr Bassett to be the new head of the department I suppose?—
if not more black marks for honored head dont you think so?

—Your letter just here— Well!— No I dont think Mr Hazen's
resignation under these circumstances melodramatic in the least—
or anything except, as he said, the only thing to do. What *is* going
to become of the place— You know it seems to me—the whole
situation—really apalling. I dont wonder that C.B. despairs— What
does Mary say? But what can anyone say! I think that the root of the
matter is that the President simply can't distinguish between whats
decent and what isn't— I'm glad that Mr Hazen is in a position
to take decided action— Poor Madame Podere-Bauer and Miss
Williams and the rest— What can they do! I'll bubble and rage more
about all this later—and if it seems outrageous to us who are so little
concerned, so little really involved—how must it seem to the people
who do really care a great deal— Mary + C.B. and the others. Next
I will bubble and boil and rage about the Nation— Improved and
enlarged!— Lets write and suggest a comic supplement.

All of your letters have been lifesaving. Its been rather a horrid
month—nearly six weeks in fact— What funny encounters with Mrs
Abbots sister—she must be odd. Any more walks with my chief?

As for me—the temperature has now got back to normal—at
least it has for 3 days and it will stay there I hope. I begin to feel a
little alive again (this disease can make you feel perfectly dead—never

knew anything like it) and I hope to have a good 2 weeks or so before the next slump comes. Dr Baldwin came yesterday + was moved to examine my lungs. They are no worse—and no better. Miss Lucy stayed in the room all the time so neither Dr Baldwin nor I attempted any general remarks. Except—to my surprise—he spoke reflectively of pneumo-thorax—with an incision. I thought he had given that up entirely. Still—despite of everything—I *am* getting stronger; theres that much on the credit side. I went out yesterday—sleighing—for the first time in 2 months. And lately (for a few days) I've dressed in the morning—and gone out for a little while (on the porch) then as well as in the afternoon. The cough is ever with me— If only I could get rid of that. But I'll be back at work next year—see if I'm not.

Maud Temple sent me a French book (Laure)— Will you thank her—Its horrid [of] me not to write myself. And must I join the Modern Lang Asn? [Modern Language Association] Its odd how these things daunt me—they are mere meaningless routine— and I simply crumple up in front of them.

I know there are a lot of other things to write about—they've been accumulating for a long time— I'll send a second installment— Give my love to L of H [Lady of House] + C.B. + Mary. How are you? You dont neglect eggs + cream I hope—

Yours A.

The brown bible only because its the only bible I have— Is it packed miles deep under things? I would send home for one but they would infallable send me an authorzied version or revised version or Modern Readers—they are all lying about the house— and the little brown one is Simon pure King James. But dont do anything thats any trouble—*please*. If its under a lot of things let me know + I'll write home with underlined directions

Miss Esther Lowenthal/ 10 West Street/ Northampton— Mass—
[forwarded to: The Bryn Mawr Club/ East 40th St near Lexington Av/ New York City]
Saranac Lake, N Y./ 6 PM/ Mar 24 1914

Northampton, Mass/ 3-30 P/ Mar 25/ 1914
11 fols. 11 pp.
[two letters from M. L. Burton, President of Smith College, to the Rev. A.
S. Crapsey, dated 13 January 1914 and 23 January 1914, enclosed]

Dear Esther— Without apology I plunge into the history of
my latest calamity. You and Mary probably know of it already at any
rate in part—Here's my account of all of it and the usual question
as trailer— Well, now whats to be done.

The enclosed letters mother sent to me, in the most casual
fashion, on Friday morning. When I read them I felt as if the sky
were tumbling down about my head. I've never been so amazed in
my life—in fact I'm still breathless. What happened evidently was
this, Dr Burton sent the first letter (dated you'll notice *Jan 13*) to
Father. Father was away and Mother instead of doing automatically
the only thing to do—namely send the letter on to me—called in Dr
Jewett asked him to consult Dr Baldwin and then write Dr Burton.
In the meanwhile Father returned, was taken into consultation—and
Dr Jewett first and then Father wrote Dr Burton definitely giving
up my position for next year. After this Father, as far as I can make
out, forgot all about the transaction and Mother put the letters away
(forgetting about them too probably!)—and by no breath or sign of
any description was it intimated to me that anything had been done.

In the meanwhile as you know my chief, through Mary, sent
me the question Dr Burton had asked father—that is how I was
getting on and what chance there was of my being at work next
year. I answered as you know—my answer being as I now discover
utter nonsense since Dr Burton already had Dr Jewetts answer
as decidedly settling everything. This Miss Jordan must also have
discovered when she reported to Dr Burton. (Its an illumination
that Dr Burton hadn't before told her that he had himself written?)
As you know I was puzzled over having nothing in answer to my
letter to Miss Jordan and then decided that it was simply because
no special action had been taken by the Trustees and that the date

I had fixed for a final decision was satisfactory. Being essentially a placid soul I let it go at that— Now its clear that Miss Jordan didn't write—because what could she write? From the two letters—Dr Jewetts and mine—it was only too apparent that while my elders and betters had decided what I was to do the decision was being "kept from" me and I was being allowed to think that I could go on (or perhaps go on) with my work by way of keeping me cheered up or heaven knows what. She (Miss Jordan) couldn't of course tell me what was being so elaborately (and so damnably) concealed—neither could she make any reply to my question (as to whether April would be too late for a decision) because as a question it had no real existence— So there she was and like a sensible woman she did nothing. Mary I think must have been in the same perdicament—since Miss Jordan problaly told her what had happened—and I fancy that Mary must have told you—

When it comes to saying what I think of the whole thing I'm simply bereft of words. It seems to me utterly unbelievably that such a decision should have been made without consulting me—and that it should then have been "kept from" me for two whole months. Now I've not only got to face what I dreaded beyond everything else—another year without work—but instead of making the decision for myself like a reasonable human being (and I knew perfectly well that such a decision loomed pretty threatenin[g]ly before me) I've just been arbitrarily sand-bagged with it. That is the worst thing that could have happened—has happened in the worst possibly way—and I feel utterly disheartened and discouraged.

Father turned up on Saturday and I've explained to him with some lucidity (though truly Esther, I wasnt horrid about it) how it all seems to me. I think I converted him to my view of the matter— But of what use is that now.

There are of course still various things that aren't clear. I'm most anxious to see Dr Baldwin and I shall most straightly ask him whether he didn't tell me because Dr Jewett and Mother asked him not to. I cant imagine his following the idiotic "keep it from her policy" for any other reason. Also I'll put to him various things that I havent yet explained— things that would have had a bearing on the question of my working next year. To Dr Baldwin, you know as to most laymen, all teaching is alike, He thinks of it, I've made out, in preparatory or high school terms. I feel pretty sure that he thinks that I must be in a class room at a given time say 8.30 or 9 and teach steadily till 4— The more flexible hours of colleg[e] in work—the whole difference in the character of the teaching— that doesnt exist for him. I haven't explained—I thought it time enough to do it when the matter came up finally—wh. [which] I expected would be this or next week. Its not, as I told Father, that I'm sure all of those things would have made a difference but that I had at any rate the right to present them for what they were worth.

However the practical politics of the affair lie now, not here, but in Northampton. You'll notice that Dr Burton's deep disappointment is that hes not to have me "another year"— What does that mean? I found that it was Father's aimiable idea that he had simply postponed my return for a year. Again I pointed out to him that what he had in effect done was to resign my position for me permanetly—since I can see no reason why it should be held open for me any longer. What is my next move—just to send in a formal resignation? Will you and Mary take consul [counsel] and let me have your light on it all

And oh, do you really think it was quite necessary to have all this happen? It gives me the most insecure, exposed feeling. From what unexpected corner will the next bolt be shot!

More later—this just a first dazed exclamation over the thing. I hope that its not shrill or excited—I've not meant it to be—that its to any extent that you please hurt and bewildered I dont pretend to deny— It seems to me so incomprehensible that anyone should have done exactly this sort of thing to exactly me.

Your nice little New York notes are here—and the netts [?] There is a new patient in the house— Love to Mary—but I'm writting her too

Wearily yours A.

All this of course for you and Mary and no one else— that is the extent to wh. [which] I feel devistated by the facts themselves— dear me, I'm the only person who hasnt known/it/them/!

I must I suppose manage a letter to Miss Jordan—and seem dimly to see myself taking, as the only way out, a slightly jocose tone—to the extent that is of some reference to the overperturbation of my family (after the way of families) etc etc—

Arrives Dr Browe [sp?]—no—man for the other patient

I've written more briefly to Mary—telling her you would arrive with these 11 pages of detail—if you both can stand it!

Miss Esther Lowenthal/ 10 West Street/Northampton— Mass Saranac Lake, N.Y./I PM/Apr 7/1914

19 May 1914
Saranac Lake, N.Y.
1 fol. 4 pp.

Dear Esther— Letter to Hon. Pres. [Honorable President] at last off— I made out check for magnif[i]cent sum of $160.00 to include May payment. Heaven send that amount really is in the bank— there is no reason why it shouldnt be but I never seem to feel sure of any of my accounts. They seem my[s]terious things. What do you say to a bank when you want them to send you your canceled checks + things? I've never had to ask the "statement" (?) has always turned up of itself but the bank here seems to need a special request. Wouldn't it have been fun to return that 200 in $20 per month installments— Why didnt I think of it—or did I once before mention so gay a project.

What about Virginia— I'm hoping you'll go. . That is if you would really get some rest and fun out of it. If I should find my new place in time to move around about Commencent time would you pay me your visit there (wherever it is it would be nearer than here) + help me settle? There is still, I may add, no tomb in sight.

If flowery dressing gowns are hard to find dont persue them. I mentioned them only because I seemed to remember seeing a lot of them last year. Yes I know—long sleeves are a vain dream— Please dont take a lot of trouble— You are not Hercules you know and this is a fairly busy time of the year—as I remember it! It seems a million billion years since I was alive and on the job—(or half alive any how).

How are you?

Yours A.

Miss Esther Lowenthal/ 10 West Street/ Northampton— Mass.
Saranac Lake, N.Y./ 6 PM/ May 19/ 1914

IMAGE GALLERY

SMITH COLLEGE

ENGLISH 3b

June, 1911

Every student is asked to take I and one or two of the topics included under II. She is expected to present her material in carefully developed form.

I.

TO SLEEP.

A flock of sheep that leisurely pass by,
    One after one ; the sound of rain, and bees
Murmuring ; the fall of rivers, winds and seas,
    Smooth fields, white sheets of water, and pure sky;
I have thought of all by turns, and yet do lie
Sleepless! and soon the small birds' melodies
Must hear, first uttered from my orchard trees ;
    And the first cuckoo's melancholy cry.
Even thus last night, and two nights more, I lay
    And could not win thee, Sleep! by any stealth :
So do not let me wear to-night away :
    Without thee what is all the morning's wealth?
Come, blessed barrier between day and day,
    Dear mother of fresh thoughts and joyous health !
                                                WORDSWORTH.

No, thou proud dream,
That play'st so subtly with a king's repose ;
I am a king that find thee and I know
'Tis not the balm, the sceptre and the ball,
The sword, the mace, the crown imperial,
The intertissued robe of gold and pearl,
The farced title running fore the king,
The throne he sits on, nor the tide of pomp
That beats upon the high shore of this world ;

A page from one of Crapsey's syllabi at Smith College for "English 3b," June 1911.

The Garden

Adelaide on lower
porch —

678 Averill Ave
Rochester N.Y.
1914

Upper porch – Where Adelaide
spent much time

Experiment in Prosodic Analysis.

In the present paper I ~~am going to give~~ am giving the results of an experimental use of a scheme of verse analysis based on the inclusion of two factors, metrical structure and phonetic speech-structure. The experiment has been carried out mainly in the analysis of verse written in duple metre (rising cadence) — English "iambic" verse — and I will give its explanation with exclusive reference to this metre. In making the explanation I am limiting myself to the briefest possible statement, and I will use, with no formal definition of them, the terms that it is most natural for me to use, trusting ~~largely~~ to the context to make them clear.

At present it seems to me that in order to understand the technique of any poem I must make an analysis both of the metrical arrangement and of the vocabulary in its phonetic structural aspect, and then, by contrasting the construction model of the metrical arrangement with the phonetic types of the vocabulary, I can see what the technical problems of the poem are, and how the artist

Charms (Cherokee Indians) —

—— (1) Love Charm —

Ku! Listen! In Hla kiyi you repose, o Terrible Woman,
O you have drawn near to hearken.
There in Elayihi you rest, o white woman.
When with you no one ever is lonely.
Most beautiful are you.
At once you have made me a white man.
When with me no one ever is lonely.
How you have made the path white for me
Never shall it be dreary.
How you have put me into it.
Never shall it become blue.
The white road you have brought down to me.
There in mid-earth you have placed one.
Upon the earth shall I stand erect.
When with me no one ever is lonely.

(Double space) } Into the white house you have led me.

There in Elayihi you have made the woman blue.
How you have made the path blue for her.
Let her be wholly veiled in loneliness.
Where her feet are now and where ever she goes
                 leave its mark
Let loneliness ~~wait upon her.~~ upon her.

Ha! I belong to the wolf clan,
~~That one alone~~ which was destined for you.
No one is ever lonely with me.
In the midst of men may she never think of them.
I belong to the one clan destined for you
when the seven clans were established.

Crapsey swinging on a hammock on the lawn at Rochester family house.

JUDY GREEN MUSIC   Hollywood, CA 90028 (213) 466-2491   T-3

Winter —

The cold
with steely grip
Clutches the land .. while
the little people on the hills
will die!

Draft of the cinquain, "Winter."

TO A NIGHTINGALE

My heart aches, and a drowsy numbness pains
  My sense, as though of hemlock I had drunk,
Or emptied some dull opiate to the drains
  One minute past, and Lethe-wards had sunk :
'Tis not through envy of thy happy lot,
  But being too happy in thy happiness,—
    That thou, light-winged Dryad of the trees,
        In some melodious plot
Of beechen green, and shadows numberless,
  Singest of summer in full-throated ease.

O for a draught of vintage, that hath been
  Cool'd a long age in the deep-delved earth,
Tasting of Flora and the country-green,
  Dance, and Provençal song, and sun-burnt mirth !
O for a beaker full of the warm South,
  Full of the true, the blushful Hippocrene,
    With beaded bubbles winking at the brim,
        And purple-stained mouth ;
That I might drink and leave the world unseen,
  And with thee fade away into the forest dim :

Fade far away, dissolve, and quite forget
  What thou among the leaves hast never known,
The weariness, the fever, and the fret
  Here, where men sit and hear each other groan ;
Where palsy shakes a few, sad, last grey hairs,
  Where youth grows pale, and spectre-thin, and dies ;
    Where but to think is to be full of sorrow
        And leaden-eyed despairs ;
Where beauty cannot keep her lustrous eyes,
  Or new Love pine at them beyond to-morrow.

49

Dear Esther— Will this do at all? Don't hesitate to say
no. It's been the devil's own week but I just went
ahead & tried anyhow— the results however are probably
fit only for the waste paper basket. Its fearfully humiliating
to have to work so hard over a perfectly simple
letter. My intellectual self respect is trailing in the
dust— Do you think I am always going to be an
idiot? It seems a sad fate. Anyhow tell me
what you think of the letter — is that enough — or
ought I to say anything more — except the polite
flourish at the end. I wonder how much flourish
is necessary in these circles. Had I do much
protesting as to Exheen & Gardner & the learned
professors (who ever he is to be) in squandering
his valuable time etc etc. I don't much like
the phrase "find a hearing for" but I wanted
something that didn't suggest a demand for

COMPRESSION AND TECHNIQUE IN ADELAIDE CRAPSEY'S CINQUAINS

Benjamin Johnson

BENJAMIN JOHNSON is a Professor of English at the University of Central Missouri. His work on modern literature has appeared in venues including MELUS, Texas Studies in Literature and Language, Arizona Quarterly, *and* The Wallace Stevens Journal, *and he co-edited the 2016 Unsung Masters book* Beatrice Hastings: On the Life & Work of a Lost Modern Master.

Adelaide Crapsey's cinquains are undoubtedly her most famous contribution to American poetry. Today, her invention of the form is the first thing mentioned in her profile on the Poetry Foundation website,[1] but even a century ago, when Louis Untermeyer selected her work for his *Modern American Poetry* anthologies, his introduction to her poems focuses on cinquains—a form he finds "saturated . . . with her own fragile loveliness"— and three of the four poems he includes are cinquains.[2] Crapsey's most famous form was also the source of her most significant publication in an avant-garde venue: thirteen of her cinquains appear in the March 1916 issue of *Others* alongside poems by Carl Sandburg, Kenneth Burke, and Wallace Stevens (including the first publication of "Domination of Black").[3] While there has never been a tremendous amount of critical ink spilled on Crapsey's work, Susan Sutton Smith notes that there have been a variety of scholarly opinions expressed about the cinquains, including arguments about whether it is useful to label them Imagist poems, whether and how they were influenced by Japanese poetry, and whether they are best defined by syllable-counts or stress-counts.[4]

And yet, for all the attention they have garnered relative to the rest of her work, there actually are not very many Adelaide Crapsey cinquains. Crapsey's *Complete Poems* contains 36 poems written according to her formula for the cinquain: five lines of metrical verse in a sequence of one foot, two feet, three feet, four feet, and then a final one foot line. Add them all together and you get 396 total feet of Crapsey cinquains, which, to put it in perspective, is roughly half the number of feet in Wordsworth's "Tintern Abbey." Even in the aggregate, Crapsey's cinquains are compact.

To appreciate the cinquains is above all else to appreciate Crapsey's ability to manage compression. Part of the excitement of reading any poem in a strict form is seeing whether the poet can make prosodic rules feel like the natural, unimprovable shape of the poem's native sounds and ideas rather than an arbitrarily imposed scaffolding, and the best of Crapsey's cinquains certainly pass that test. But they gain an extra drama from their brevity. With only eleven metrical feet with which to work, every technical choice Crapsey makes is magnified: the calculated disruption of flow from having multiple commas in a line; the tension of a verb on an enjambed line break; the scrape of a single instance of alliteration. Crapsey's major poetry was written in a narrow window from about 1910 to 1914, and like many poems from this period by Pound, H.D., Flint, and other writers of the Imagist group, Crapsey's cinquains work through an aesthetic of brevity that at its best allows for poems that are both impressionistic and taut. But unlike the vast majority of Imagist poetry, Crapsey's cinquains hew very closely to English traditions of accentual-syllabic scansion, and indeed, always lean to the iamb as their predominant foot. Crapsey composes in the "sequence of a metronome" at the precise moment that the Imagists were decrying the practice,[5] and her cinquains often present pocket-sized human melodramas rather than the austere landscapes of H.D.'s *Sea Garden*. In some ways her work correlates to high Modernism, but she certainly was not caused by it, and her cinquains read at a century's remove like an attempt to design personalized constraints that will allow her to construct 11-foot workshops of poetic technique.

To my ear, the most impressive technical achievement in Crapsey's cinquains is her management of pace. Crapsey frequently uses internal punctuation to slow lines, but this works in tension with the inherent structure of the cinquain form, which tends to feel restless because its atypically high number of line breaks per foot[6] necessitates a great deal of enjambment. This combination allows her best cinquains to push and pull in concert with the sturm und drang of their subject matter. "November Night" has pride of place as the first poem in the selection of her work in *Others*, and it is an excellent example of Crapsey's ability to use pauses for dramatic effect:

> Listen . . .
> With faint dry sound,
> Like steps of passing ghosts,
> The leaves, frost-crisp'd, break from the trees
> And fall.

It is actually quite rare in the cinquains for Crapsey's clauses to hew so closely to her line lengths, but they do here, as she opens with three end-stopped lines of one, two, and three feet. The pauses underscore the speaker's demand for cautious observation. It reads as though the poem itself does not want to make any abrupt, distracting movements, even as the metrical variations of the first two lines make the poem feel restless (a trochee, iamb, and spondee are the first three feet). The third line is entirely iambic, perhaps to mimic the "steps of passing ghosts," but its regularity is just a set-up for the much more sonically complex fourth line. The first half of the fourth line is incredibly slow, with pauses after the first and second feet, and the second foot is the consonant-dense spondee "frost-crisp'd." The entire fourth line seems to crunch, as an "r" sound runs through the background as the second part of a consonant cluster in five of the last six words. And then, after all that sonic density, we get the first moment of enjambment in the poem, which fittingly leaves us dangling for a climactic moment before we reach "And fall" in the final line of the poem. There is nothing inherently dramatic in the autumnal scene that Crapsey describes; indeed, as I am writing this in early November, leaves are falling all over my midwestern backyard and the primary emotion I experience in watching them is resigned annoyance. But Crapsey is able to convey a miniature drama in "November Night" entirely because of her application of a few precise brushstrokes of poetic technique.

In "Niagara Seen on a Night in November" Crapsey essentially reverses the pace of "November Night," as this poem begins in a rush before slowing at the conclusion:

> How frail
> Above the bulk
> Of crashing water hangs,
> Autumnal, evanescent, wan,
> The moon.

Again the poem is only one sentence long, but unlike "November Night" the first clause lasts six full metrical feet and extends across two enjambed line endings to fill the first three lines. The most dramatic effect Crapsey achieves in the poem, however, comes from her decision to separate the verb ("hangs") and subject ("moon") by a tetrameter line consisting entirely of adjectives. We are left, like the moon, to hang through an entire, pause-heavy line that carefully describes a grammatical subject which remains hidden until we arrive at the final word of the sentence (and poem). Many if not most of Crapsey's cinquains evoke a sense of meditative calm, but this is especially true of this poem, as the speaker stands before the "bulk / of crashing water" that is Niagara Falls, focusing her attention not on the sublime chaos of the waterfall, but the frailty of the pale, silent moon. The insistence with which that fourth line makes us wait for the moon to appear only adds to its air of stately silence. "November Night" begins with control and ends in a tumble; "Niagara Seen on a Night in November" begins by impelling us forward and ends by stopping us short. Nonetheless, both poems succeed above all else because of Crapsey's ability to manage the pace at which we proceed through the lines.

Poetic techniques related to sound repetition are also significant in the cinquains, and this is especially apparent in "Madness" and "Lunatick," two poems which, as the titles suggest, share a common topic. "Madness" is probably the better poem of the two:

> Burdock,
> Blue aconite,
> And thistle and thorn . . . of these,
> Singing I wreathe my pretty wreath
> O'death.

Death is a frequent topic of the cinquains, but rarely is death quite so stylized as it is here, as Crapsey wreaths together a list of poisonous plants (burdock, blue aconite) and the parts of plants that are potentially painful to the unwary botanist ("thistle and thorn"). "Madness" recalls *Hamlet*, specifically the end of Act IV, Scene 5 where Ophelia, lost to madness, sings and hands out flowers in her last onstage appearance prior to her drowning. Crapsey's speaker and Ophelia are both performatively feminine, even girlish, in their tuneful naming and placing of plants, but where Shakespeare uses Ophelia's obliviousness to other characters to convey the eeriness of her behavior, Crapsey, with much less space at her disposal, unsettles the reader with the inherent menace of the dangerous objects in her speaker's "wreath / O'death." The alliteration in the poem is "pretty" but also discomfiting: the first two lines open with concussive "b" sounds, but then the second part of the poem has a slithery undercurrent due to the "th" sounds that begin three words of line three, and end three words in lines four and five.

The alliterative poisonous plants that begin the poem are obvious attention-grabbers, but the mention of "thistle and thorn" in line three connects Crapsey to a wide array of modernist poets who reimagined the flower poem around themes of hardness or toughness: William Carlos Williams's "The Rose" and H.D.'s various sea-flower poems spring to mind, but Crapsey's "Madness" especially recalls Marianne Moore's concluding assertion in "Roses Only" that "your thorns are the best part of you."[7] Crapsey's "Madness" differs, though, from the American high Modernist reinvention of the flower poem. Moore, Williams, and H.D. tend to abandon or mock the traditional association of flowers and femininity in English poetry ("You do not seem to realise that beauty is a liability rather than / an asset," writes Moore), but Crapsey, with her evocation of singing Ophelia amidst the "thistles and thorns" that sit in the middle of the poem, crafts a poem that is jarring because it unites girlishness and menace.

In "Lunatick," Crapsey puts a spin on the theme of madness by using second-person to suggest that perhaps the reader ("thou" is the only human mentioned in the poem) is the lunatic of the title:

> Dost thou
> Not feel them slip,
> How cold! how cold! the moon's
> Thin wavering finger-tips along
> Thy throat?

As in "November Night," Crapsey uses pauses and syntactic delay to build tension. After "slip," the poem pauses after three consecutive feet before allowing the reader to discover what it is that is slipping (and where). The most interesting sonic moment in the poem, though, is the internal rhyme of "slip" and "tips"— two words that connect not only sonically but also in the plot of the poem. The unexpected rhyme is particularly impactful since it links the third and ninth feet of the poem, which causes our ear to hear the lines as though they were rhyming endings of the first and third lines in an iambic trimeter poem. If we hear the poem this way, we might have an aural expectation of a fourth trimeter line, but instead we only get two more feet before the poem (and the moon's fingertips) arrives at the reader's throat. Crapsey always has an ability to convey a dark, brooding, and even spooky mood in her poems, but "Lunatick" is also quite clever: in the way it plays with sound and in the pun buried in the title ("lunatic" being derived from the Latin, "luna").

The range of effects Crapsey achieves in her cinquains is impressive. "Night Winds" and "Arbutus," for instance, are both about nature, though they move in very different ways. "Night Winds" is fast and bombastic, with only a single pause roughly halfway through the poem (a comma after the second foot of the third line). In addition to its speed, Crapsey adds to the sense of energy in the poem with a repeated word over the first line break ("The old / Old winds"), and long vowel sounds on the last four line endings ("blew," "do," "I," "weep"). "Arbutus," on the other hand, has six commas in the second through fourth lines of the poem, and a hyphenated adjective ("Rose-tinged") that slows the final line. Between these two poems, I prefer "Arbutus." I generally find Crapsey's cinquains to be at their best when the lines are clotted with pauses and stresses (as previously discussed with "November Night"), but across the whole range of her cinquains, she uses the concentrated medium to test out a variety of techniques.

The Adelaide Crapsey archive at the University of Rochester contains several manuscripts of cinquains that demonstrate just how carefully Crapsey weighed her various poetic decisions. Take, for instance, "Winter," which in the published versions in both *Others* and *The Complete Poems* begins, "The cold / With steely clutch / Grips all the land." However, a handwritten manuscript version in the Rochester files begins "The cold / With steely grip / Clutches the land."[8] Interestingly, Crapsey has scanned the lines in her handwritten manuscript (something she did with some frequency), so it is likely that rhythm is at least part of her concern in her editing process. In the manuscript version, everything is iambic except the trochee "Clutches." When "Clutches" changes to "Grips all," however, the foot becomes trickier to scan (an auditor could hear it either as a spondee or an iamb). Regardless, "clutch / Grips all" is more difficult to speak than "grip / Clutches." As a result, the final, published version slows the poem down at the start of line three, which is vital, given that the action being described is grabbing. The other effect of swapping the syllable "es" for "all" is that Crapsey builds on the alliteration on the letter "l" that runs through the entire poem.

The Rochester archive also has manuscript variants for the poem "Snow." In its finished version, it is one of Crapsey's stronger cinquains, and certainly one that showcases her ability to use alliteration and heavy pauses to build a sense of drama in a nature poem:

> Look up . . .
> From bleakening hills
> Blows down the light, first breath
> Of wintry wind . . . look up, and scent
> The snow!

Crapsey's alliteration is lovely in this poem, as a predominance of "l" and "b" sounds in the early lines gives way to "w" and "s" sounds at the conclusion. The poem has a dark, sublime feel that emerges from its "bleakening hills," and it invokes multiple senses, as the reader is twice commanded to "look up" and once commanded to "scent / The snow." The key word in the poem is "bleakening"—it sits in the middle of the second line and casts a dark pall over what might otherwise seem a uniformly pleasant scene. It is also, significantly, a word Crapsey has more or less willed into being, since I am not able to find "bleaken" or "bleakening" in any dictionary. The manuscripts of the poem reveal that it took her a while to arrive at the word "bleakening."[9] In her drafts, Crapsey originally wrote "Look up! / The first," and then crossed out "first" to replace it with "keen." This led her to trying out "Look up / The keen first breath" and "Look up / With sudden breath / The keen and wintry wind."[10] There are also several other, shorter false starts to the poem on this page of the manuscript, but what strikes me here is the word "keen," which does not appear in the final version of the poem even though Crapsey clearly took several stabs at making it work. It is tempting to speculate that the long "e" of "keen" led her to the sonically similar "bleak." Regardless, "keen" would be less effective in the poem than "bleakening," since the most powerful thing about "Snow" is Crapsey's evocation of winter weather that rolls down out of the hills not like a keen knife edge, but as a spreading, permeating, inescapable presence that we initially "scent" rather than see.

Crapsey's cinquains are a fascinating example of the trend toward brevity and compression that defined much important American poetry of the early 1910s, and they are important historically for revealing that this trend was not limited to the free verse poetics that have dominated anthology selections from this period for decades. There are certainly commonalities between the best cinquains, most notably that the longer fourth line tends to be where Crapsey's sonic inventiveness with pause and alliteration comes to the fore, and also that the poems' success or failure often hinges on how well she manages the drop into the inevitably conspicuous single foot of the final line. But despite the inherent similarities of poems in a strict, compressed form, the best of the cinquains stand alone, and have for too long been missing from histories of twentieth-century poetics.

NOTES

1 https://www.poetryfoundation.org/poets/adelaide-crapsey

2 Louis Untermeyer, *Modern American Poetry* (New York: Harcourt, Brace, and Company, 1921), 206.

3 Adelaide Crapsey, "Cinquains," *Others* (Vol. 2, No. 3), March 1916. 1679.

4 Smith's Introduction to *The Complete Poems & Collected Letters of Adelaide Crapsey* provides an excellent rundown of these arguments. See especially pp. 23-9.

5 F.S. Flint, "Imagisme," *Poetry* (Vol. 1, No. 6), March 1913, 199.

6 Four of the eleven feet in a cinquain (36%) precede a non-terminal line break, which is a very high number compared to most formal English verse.

7 Marianne Moore, "Roses Only," *Becoming Marianne Moore: The Early Poems, 1907-24* (Berkeley, U of California Press, 2002): 83.

8 "Winter," Adelaide Crapsey Papers, University of Rochester, Box 2, File 2, A.C89.

9 "Snow," Adelaide Crapsey Papers, University of Rochester, Box 2, File 2, A.C89.

10 I'm not fully confident that "The" is the first word of the third line in this particular draft, but it is my best guess at interpreting Crapsey's handwriting.

DEATH BECOMES HER: ADELAIDE CRAPSEY'S EMERGING VOICE IN "TO THE DEAD IN THE GRAVEYARD UNDERNEATH MY WINDOW"

Erin Adair-Hodges

ERIN ADAIR-HODGES is the author of Let's All Die Happy, *winner of the 2016 Agnes Lynch Starrett Poetry Prize. She is currently a visiting professor of creative writing at the University of Toledo in Ohio.*

Adelaide Crapsey—when she is remembered at all—is rarely noted for her humor. Crapsey biographer Edward Butscher describes her late poems' "thematic obsession with death"[1], which is true and also grossly unfair. Many poets are obsessed with death, and with far less reason. Crapsey endured debilitating sickness for much of her adult life; it made the life she wanted to live, one filled with studying and writing and teaching, nearly impossible. That we have any work from her at all is testament to her tenacity, filled with a preoccupation with death or not.

To be so young, talented, and sick is the stuff of great tragedy, understating the challenge of viewing her poems outside this context. Perhaps we don't need to—once a poet's biography is learned, it can't be unlearned, so it's intellectually dishonest to pretend otherwise. Rather, it is fairer to remember that a poet's work is informed by, but not necessarily about, their circumstances. Crapsey's terminal illness, along with the loss of several of her siblings, pivoted her toward death, not as the "obsession" that Butscher describes, but rather an inevitability, one coming unbearably soon.

Understanding this, two interesting points emerge: the first is that while a good number of Crapsey's poems deal with death, they do not necessarily deal with *her* death. This is of course not out of line of the post-Romantic, pre-Imagist tradition Crapsey trucked in: confessional poetry was a couple of world wars away from its advent. Further, Crapsey died less than three months after the beginning of World War I and years from the United States' entrance into it, so in many ways, she was leaving a world that would soon no longer exist. There is then, in much of her work, a turning toward Eternal Themes, Universals, Capital Letters Intended. There's a sense in those poems concerning death that they are also dealing with Death (Death in the Tragic sense, Death not coming for each body named and loved by someone but Death with a hood—Death with a cawl and waiting for us all); unfortunate certainly but which should also be faced bravely. The carnage wrought by the Great War would change Western views of young death, moving it from the stuff of the Romantics to brutal waste. Crapsey, of course, would know nothing of this, and in some ways what she gives us are the final glimpses of an Anglopoetic handling of death as alternately quasi-gothic and noble.

We see this shift in attitudes towards death in the evolution of poetry on the war, beginning with poems like Rupert Brooke's 1914 poem "The Soldier," with lines like "If I should die, think only this of me: / That there's some corner of a foreign field / That is for ever England."[2] By 1918, poems such as "God! How I hate you, you young cheerful men" by Arthur Graeme West and Wilfred Owen's indelible "Dulce et Decorum Est" underscore the idea that there is nothing to be celebrated or even learned from untimely death—it is barbarism and it is waste.

That we, as modern readers, know what would be coming so soon after her death does not help us understand Crapsey's composition, though—she was not gifted with foresight, or perhaps even, because of the intensity of the end stages of her tuberculosis, an awareness of the events unfolding an ocean away. Her letters to friends and family almost completely stop in the spring of 1914, and the few she does write after that are filled with small requests and apologies for the inconvenience of her illness.

Instead, we see in Crapsey's late poems (both those included in *Verse* and those uncollected), a treatment of Death as a universal, inevitable part of human experience, and less a poet's grappling with the emotional landscape of understanding her own imminent demise. One of Crapsey's best-known cinquains, "Triad," is a prime example of this:

> These be
> Three silent things:
> The falling snow. .the hour
> Before the dawn. .the mouth of one
> Just dead.[3]

Here, in one of her most effective uses of her invented form, we see a depiction of happenings as hushed around: one in the moment of, one in the moment before, and finally the silence of the moment after. It is also a portrait of transitions; "one / Just dead" is also necessarily one who was just living, an indication of the photo through the presentation of its negative. But it is also a poem about Death, any death, all death: hers, yours, mine.

Even in poems that employ an "I" as the supposed experiencer and observer, the first-person functions as a device, a pronoun to put a human body in so as to have a voice with authority. In another cinquain, "Moon-shadows," the "I" is less the locus for experience than a tool that provides a turn:

> Still as
> On windless nights
> The moon-cast shadows are,
> So still will be my heart when I
> Am dead.[4]

Read without knowing Crapsey's biography, there is nothing here to indicate the expression of any particular anxiety over death, or rather, anxiety over any particular death. If the old saying about poetry is true, that all of it is either about sex or death, it's no surprise to see a poem use the latter as muse. Instead, we see a clever feint where, in a move similar to that in "Triad," our consideration of the natural world is used to help us understand impermanence, the shuffling toward our own stillness.

Even in one of her more sustained employments of the first-person (outside persona poems such as "The Crucifixion") in "The Lonely Death," we are encouraged to see the "I" as indicating what all of us will experience:

> In the cold I will rise, I will bathe
> In waters of ice; myself
> Will shiver, and shrive myself,
> Alone in the dawn, and anoint
> Forehead and feet and hands;
> I will shutter the windows from light,
> I will place in their sockets the four
> Tall candles and set them a-flame
> In the grey of the dawn; and myself
> Will lay myself straight in my bed,
> And draw the sheet under my chin.[5]

There is much that is striking about this poem. Crapsey's best work displays a keen sense of pacing, and here we see it is only in the final two lines where all that has been prepared for finally being realized. There is also an interesting repetition of "myself," which often indicates one's spirit or separate consciousness, but here every reference is to the physical body, underscoring that while our understanding of our "selves" varies wildly, what we hold in common is that we are tethered to bodies, and that regardless of how much we are loved, the journey of leaving those bodies is one we take alone.

It does not take away from Crapsey's artistry or unique voice to say she worked within the tradition of her time and place in her treatment of humanity's, and therefore poetry's, primary concerns. It can, however, help us appreciate the notable departures from her presentation of Universal Death, variances which give us a peek into the emergence of a singular poetic voice.

The most significant example of this can be found in "To the Dead in the Graveyard Underneath My Window," written in November 1913. The first swerving away from her more typical treatments of death comes immediately in the title, which Crapsey biographer Butscher sees as a "branch of the modernist stream that had its source in Whitman (and perhaps Dickinson)."[6] And though he certainly misses the mark on other aspects (such as bemoaning the "technical prissiness" of "The Lonely Death"),[7] there is something true in how he sees the title functioning. Its expansiveness could be seen as a relinquishment of some of Crapsey's trademark control, but it also varies in drawing a distinction between the speaker and the dead—different from the poems in which the speaker is often more of a soon-dead voice aligned with the deceased.

Significant also is Crapsey's employment of the first person in this poem, which is distinct from nearly any other usage of "I" in her work. The I here isn't the Poet; it's not a device or a mask—it is as near to the voice of Adelaide Crapsey as we have in any of her poems. In fact, it sounds much more like the Adelaide of her letters:

clever and frustrated not just by death, but that its slow approach is making living so much harder. The poem is even subtitled *written in a moment of exasperation*, and it seems as if the imposed listlessness brought by fatal illness wore away Crapsey's standard approaches to what couldn't help but be her main concern.

The poem begins with a short question—"How can you lie so still?"[8] Yet in its placement at the beginning, prefacing a long, winding 11-line sentence, it becomes an accusation. This is not a rhetorical move to have us consider the nature of death; it's an indictment of the dead. The poem goes on in that first line:

> . . . All day I watch
> And never a blade of all the green sod moves
> To show where restlessly you toss and turn,
> And fling a desperate arm or draw up knees
> Stiffened and aching from their long disuse.

The "I" here emerges as a singular person speaking to specific experience, that of a keen-eyed invalid hungry for action, limited from her own physical exertions and angry to see other bodies succumb, with no restless desperation evident. The title locates us in an actual place: a room in a house with a window, a real person at the glass.

With no energy or resources herself, the speaker goes on:

> I watch all night and not one ghost comes forth
> To take its freedom of the midnight hour.
> Oh, have you no rebellion in your bones?
> The very worms must scorn you where you lie,
> A pallid mouldering acquiescent folk,
> Meek habitants of unresented graves.

The speaker of these lines watches day and night, prevented from doing anything else, forced into acute perception:

> Where I must ever see you from my bed
> That in your mere dumb presence iterate
> The text so weary in my ears: "Lie still
> And rest; be patient and lie still and rest." (13-16)

We're encouraged to see this as a personal "I" (near-confessional, for want of a better term), located in physical time and space, recipient to specific and infuriating advice. In this poem, Crapsey moves from a treatment of Death into a forced consideration of her own death, for while we will all die, we won't all be invalids. We won't all be told in our youth to spend our days and nights in bed, hoping stillness will cure or at least halt disease's creep. And so then the speaker's rejoinder to this advice—"I'll not be patient! I will not lie still!"—works not only as a moving turn in the poem: it also serves as an indicator of Crapsey's move from a meticulously constructed poetic voice into something modern readers might recognize as more authentic.

This is not to argue that poetic authenticity is bound up with the employment of first-person or the revelation of autobiographical details. Rather, this sense of authenticity comes from the feeling that the poet has risked something in the writing of this poem. The poem is still emblematic of Crapsey's attention to stresses and rhythm—it's largely in iambic pentameter, with notable variations such as "Meek habitants of unresented graves" recalling Whitman and the contemporaneous work of Carl Sandburg. The variation, then, comes not in form or image but in voice: singular, belonging to one person in one broken body refusing to go gently into the good night.

And yet the speaker is not foolish enough to think that attitude will defeat death. The second instance of the poem's rebellious declaration removes the exclamation points: "I'll not be patient. I will not lie still." We can see this as a gritty determination, a promise rather than the impassioned (though never hysterical) cries of the previous uttering. And it is this, but it also comes at the end of the poem's first, long (40 lines) stanza before the final eight-line stanza, which understands that regardless of how spirited the sick may be, death wins, making its "Grim casual comment on rebellion's end / 'Yes; yes . . . *Wilfil and petulant but now / As dead and quiet as the others are.*"

It's tempting to see the two stanzas as indicative of Crapsey's two voices: the passionate personal and the studied poetic. The first stanza could stand on its own, a wholly complete treatment on how exasperating and stupid dying is for the speaker. The second stanza, though, reverts back to Crapsey's more typical treatment of death, as the universal stage manager tasked with ending all of our plays. Gone is the singular first-person—the only instance of any first-person in this stanza comes in one plural: "And in ironic quietude who is / the despot of our days and lord of dust." The "I" that raged against stillness has left behind a speaker considering the triumph of Death over us all.

This move may not be an abandonment of the prior stanza's divergent voice; it could be a move we see in plenty of contemporary poetry, the positing of personal experience as having resonance and meaning beyond the self. Perhaps this urge was (and is) especially strong for women writers like Crapsey, who were never able to see their experiences as default or normative, and we see even today distrust of a female "I." Or maybe it was simply the emergence of Crapsey's education and inclination, guiding the poem back to familiar philosophical ground.

Despite the "why" of the poem's move, it serves to reveal through contrast how atypical the bulk of the poem is, how remarkable. To the dead, this dying speaker proclaims:

> Recumbent as you others must I too
> Submit? Be mimic of your movelessness
> With pillow and counterpane for stone and sod?
> And if the many sayings of the wise
> Teach of submission I will not submit
> But with a spirit all unreconciled
> Flash an unquenched defiance to the stars.

Two exciting points emerge in this section, which follows the exclamation in the middle of the first stanza. First, it is a rejection of inculcation, of pedantic wisdom about behavior. This is a speaker who is tired of that, feels misled by that, who rebels intellectually and emotionally (if not physically) in spectacular fashion. Secondly, we see here, and in the entire poem, an unavoidable and crucial truth: this speaker is not just obsessed with death. This speaker is dying. We don't see that in Crapsey's other work, with their use of narrative distance and persona. Perhaps this is proto-confessional: I am dying, she says, and I don't want to be.

We can't know if the emergence of this voice would have been something Crapsey would continue to explore or if it was simply evidence of illness driving her to the poem's "moment of exasperation." "To the Dead in the Graveyard Underneath My Window" was written in the last year of her life, the final six months during which she wrote almost nothing, even letters. Whether it is a new path or an aberration, this poem, read within the context of her other work, reveals a poet whose unfortunate condition made her a student, and then an expert, on death. In finally writing about her own death, she is able to construct something true and unbearably alive.

NOTES

1   Edward Butscher, *Adelaide Crapsey,* (Twayne, 1979), 92.
2   Rupert Brooke, "The Soldier," *Poetry Foundation,* poetryfoundation.org.
3   Adelaide Crapsey, *The Complete Poems and Collected Letters of Adelaide Crapsey,* (Albany, State University of New York, 1977), 70.
4   Ibid., 71.
5   Ibid., 96.
6   Butscher, *Adelaide Crapsey,* 92.
7   Ibid., 94.
8   Crapsey, *Complete Poems,* 101.

COUNTING WITH CRAPSEY

Erin Kappeler

ERIN KAPPELER is Assistant Professor of English at Missouri State University, where she teaches courses in American literature. Her work has appeared in Modernism/modernity, *the* Wiley-Blackwell Companion to Modernist Poetry, *and the edited collection* Critical Rhythm, *forthcoming from Fordham University Press.*

Since its posthumous publication in 1918, Adelaide Crapsey's *A Study in English Metrics* has posed a challenge for critics, who tend to read this compact prosodic treatise as idiosyncratic and exceptional. Writing in 1923, Llewelyn Jones, for instance, argued that *A Study in English Metrics* was "perhaps unique among such studies in that it takes the great body of metrical knowledge, sifts from it the essentials, and builds from them,"[1] while Crapsey's most careful scholarly reader, Karen Alkalay-Gut, argues that Crapsey's *Study*, "in concern and approach . . . [was] utterly unlike anything else written in her time" and that her "theories of rhythm and stress were entirely original."[2] But this critical focus on Crapsey's exceptionalism does a disservice to her intense engagement with the huge body of prosodical discourse that saturated the cultural landscape of the late nineteenth and early twentieth centuries, and to her role in modernist poetics. This essay thus takes on the modest but consequential goal of reorienting Crapsey scholarship away from the image of a woman theorizing new approaches to prosody in isolation toward the image of a scholar engaged in critical conversations, writing herself into discursive fields and helping to further debates about English prosody in productive and innovative—if not entirely unique—ways.[3]

The time is ripe for a fresh analysis of Crapsey's prosodic scholarship. New work in the field of historical poetics has helped to bring back into view both the cultural ubiquity and the enormity of turn-of-the-century debates about poetic meters in English, as well as the reasons why we have forgotten that these debates happened.[4] Meredith Martin's pathbreaking *The Rise and Fall of Meter*, for instance, investigates "the historical moment when our concept of 'English meter' seems to stabilize" into a foot-based accentual-syllabic system, roughly 1860 to 1930, in order to show that "the desire for a stable and regular prosody was often complicated by the unstable way that these terms ('prosody,' 'meter,' 'versification') circulated."[5] Though we tend to take it for granted now that foot-based prosody is natural to English, Martin shows that poets and prosodists experimented fruitfully with syllabic prosody, accentual prosody, musical scansion, and other alternatives to foot-based accentual-syllabic prosody throughout this crucial period and into the present day. But because we often do take "meter," "rhythm," "prosody," "versification," and associated terms to be more or less stable now, especially in teaching texts, it can be difficult to understand just how radically these terms have shifted historically, as well as to appreciate the high stakes poets and prosodists attached to the project of stabilizing these various terms. Martin shows us that debates about prosody were almost always also debates about national and cultural identity, highlighting the need to question, "when poets were inventing or experimenting with prosodic systems, with what else, in addition to the measure of the line, were they wrestling?"[6]

In Crapsey's case, she was wrestling with the exciting notion that advances in the relatively new science of phonetics were finally making it possible for poets to understand something close to the full complexity of poetic structures in all their variety. Crapsey undertook her study at a time when prosodic theorists were working to make prosody seem "more and more like a grammar with applicable and clear rules," even as it remained clear that those seemingly set rules were affected by variations in pronunciation.[7] Earlier debates about whether prosody was essentially a matter for the eye (a textual phenomenon) or the ear (a guide to proper pronunciation) were elided in prosodic handbooks as the nineteenth century progressed,[8] and an uptick in laboratory experiments aimed at recording and parsing poetic rhythm helped to make it seem that breakthroughs in understanding the basic units of poetic rhythm and meter were finally at hand.[9] For many modernist poets and prosodists, these developments seemed to simplify the complications of prosodic debates, offering a view of prosody as a coherent and consistent system. Amy Lowell, for instance, argued that the laboratory experiments she participated in with Dr. William Patterson at Columbia University had proved once and for all that "verse . . . and prose have a different mechanical base," and had also proved that, "as the 'foot' is the unit of 'regular verse'," so was the "time unit" the basis of free verse, which Patterson had shown to consist of "several different" classifiable forms.[10] To Lowell, these conclusions were definitive; as she put it, "I fail to see how any thoughtful person can discard these divisions which Dr. Patterson has been at such pains to discover. To me, they clear up much which had hitherto remained dark."[11] Crapsey, however, saw in the turn to lab-based approaches to prosody a sign that approaches to poetic structure were about to get more complex and various rather than less. Though Crapsey believed that certain prosodic terms were being better understood and hence becoming more stable, in other words, she also believed that the stability of terms wouldn't necessarily result in a reduction of complications within prosodic analysis.

In this assessment, Crapsey was following eminent poet and critic Robert Bridges, a touchstone in her writing on prosody. Bridges was committed to understanding meter as multiplicitous, right down to its potential fundamental bases. Bridges wanted to explore the depth, complexity, and multiplicity of English meter, and consistently pushed to expand the sense of what it meant to measure verse. Bridges's conviction that prosodic systems needed to be understood as complex and various came in part from his influential work on Milton's meters, begun in the 1880s and extending through multiple editions of *Milton's Prosody* in the 1910s and 1920s. Bridges argued that a careful study of Milton's poetry showed that Milton's "use of meter adhere[d] to his . . . own laws rather than a larger, inherent design in the language."[12] Because of this, the basis of Milton's prosody could shift from poem to poem, as Bridges believed it did from *Paradise Lost* (constructed on a syllabic basis) to *Samson Agonistes* (which displayed a stress-based metrical pattern). By paying attention to how poets exploited the multiple possibilities available to them, Bridges hoped to "redee[m] Milton as well as English meter from a simple, conventional understanding of metrical form associated with rhythmic regularity."[13] If the prosodical system an author used could change from poem to poem, then prosodic theorists needed a more capacious understanding of what English meters could be.

Though Bridges's capacious approach to prosody can seem like a highly specialized intervention in a technical conversation about aesthetic choices, the social and political stakes of his project were high. Bridges was writing in response to both Edwin Guest, an Anglo-Saxonist who believed that prosody needed to be rooted in stress-based accentual verse because the proper foundation for Englishness was Anglo-Saxon culture, and George Saintsbury, who wanted to abstract classical prosody into an idea of English foot-based meters that preserved class-based educational distinctions. As Martin reminds us, "competing histories of prosody in the late nineteenth century were also competing histories of Englishness."[14] Bridges wanted it all ways, emphasizing cultural plurality rather than purity; he believed that "the purity, diversity, and freedom of English meter meant understanding each distinct possibility (the accentual, the syllabic, etc.) as a separate system that required its own kind of training and its own possibility for mastery."[15]

In *A Study in English Metrics*, Crapsey showed herself to be an astute student of Bridges who understood what was at stake in the differences between Bridges's approach to prosody and Saintsbury's. She argued that Saintsbury was the key representative of what she claimed was the first, underdeveloped stage of the study of prosody, in which theorists "think of verse as a simple uncomplex whole." In Saintsbury's case, she argued, his exclusive focus on poetic feet, or "the arrangement of syllables by means of which the rhythm is exteriorized," made him search for the rules of verse without considering how speech patterns interplayed with verse patterns.[16] Poetic feet were only one variable in verse structures, according to Crapsey, and Saintsbury's overemphasis of that one variable would lead critics to incorrect conclusions about how to evaluate different poets and how to think of what she called the "great main line of development in English poetry,"[17] and hence of Anglo-American culture.

Crapsey believed that the emerging science of linguistics could help prosodists to develop more complex, nuanced theories of poetic form, especially if prosodists worked to better understand what she saw as the two fundamental components of poetic structures: "the verse form proper, itself two-fold, consisting of (a) the rhythmic arrangement and (b) the syllabic arrangement by means of which the rhythm is exteriorized"; and the "sub-structural phonetic speech-arrangement," or "everything connected with the organized physical material of the language."[18] She argued that the word "in its phonetic aspect [is] the basic structural unit of language physically considered as the foot is the basic structural unit of the verse-form proper,"[19] meaning that any thorough prosodical analysis had to account for both the structure of the English language and the structure of poetic form. Syllables and feet had to be analyzed together, in other words, as parts of interlocking linguistic and literary systems. Such an approach would allow theorists to explore the possibilities of syllabic forms rather than exclusively focusing on accentual-syllabic or foot-based meters, thus opening up avenues of experimentation for poets while still systematizing the classification of various types of poetry.[20]

Crapsey's enthusiasm for lab-based approaches to prosody shows that she kept her finger on the pulse of prosodic discourse. Like many of her contemporaries, she argued that it was "no longer possible to discuss except on the basis of relevant evidence gathered by genuinely scientific laboratory analysis such fundamental questions of verse," and that the time had come to make "a first application of experimental phonetics to prosodic study."[21] Crapsey was writing during "a period of intense 'experimental investigation of the perception of rhythm',"[22] and she echoed calls to use experimental science as a means to better understand poetic form. Unlike many of her contemporaries, however, Crapsey didn't see rhythm as the answer to prosodical questions, but rather as one constitutive element among many in poetic form. She argued that prosodists had to work against "a tendency to throw very great emphasis on the newly observed factor" as approaches to prosody developed, with the "newly observed factor" in the early 1900s being rhythm. Crapsey argued that an overemphasis on rhythm (or on any one linguistic or poetic factor) would result in an oversimplification of the complexity of poetic form. Too, Crapsey argued, an overemphasis on rhythm specifically led prosodists to take the metaphorical comparison of poetic and musical rhythm as literal. She saw in the attempts of so-called "musical scansionists," or theorists who sought to mark poetic rhythm using musical notation, an "attempt to transfer the terms and notation developed in relation to the manifestations of a rhythm in one material to its manifestations in a different material." According to Crapsey, this was a flawed approach that resulted in a "reversion toward the primitive view of verse as an uncomplex whole."[23] Crapsey thus sought to balance attention to what she saw as the tangible material of language—syllables or phonemes—with the more abstracted notion of poetic rhythm, without confusing the relationships between the two.

Though she cautioned against placing too much focus on rhythm, Crapsey argued that the new laboratory approaches to language did allow for advances in prosodic study that required the development of more complex methods of metrical analysis. She argued that this wouldn't be something that would emerge suddenly: musical scansion was "an attempt to meet this need" for "a method allowing the close study of the rhythmic groups of verse," but that failed to do so. She saw musical scansion as the second stage in the development of prosody as a field of study, in which theorists sought to show that "what had seemed to be an uncomplex whole [was instead] . . . a complex entity containing within itself two inter-existent entities."[24] Crapsey saw the limit to this method—indeed, to all prior methods of scansion–as the limits of human perception: "What has now become apparent is that we soon reach here the limits of possible analysis based on simple observation 'by ear' or by our 'sense of rhythm'. The delicate and accurate study of the rhythmic groups of verse must, it is seen, be carried on by means of laboratory experiment."[25] Crapsey refers the age-old question of whether prosody was meant to guide vocal performance ("observation 'by ear'") or whether it was a textual form appealing primarily to the eye, to the laboratory, where the discovery of the units of rhythms could perhaps show how the two poles interacted.

Though Crapsey didn't think that laboratory-based phonetics offered the ultimate solution to the unresolved (and perhaps ultimately irresolvable) questions of how to approach prosody as a complex system, she did argue that it provided a path to what she labeled as the third stage in English prosody. Crapsey wrote that the "continued introspective analysis of our reaction to verse-structure as a whole will result in conscious awareness of the existence within it of the sub-structural speech arrangement."[26] She cited Bridges's "Rules of Stress Rhythm," which argued against the idea of verse-specific stress patterns and for the idea that stress should be "natural," as spoken, as evidence of "a growing awareness of the speech-arrangement *per se*, manifesting at the same time exactly the over-emphasis on this arrangement which would naturally accompany its first conscious perception."[27] Phonetics, in other words, had paved the way for prosodists to recognize the "non-coincidence" of speech patterns and poetic structures,[28] or the simultaneous existence of prosody as a vocal guide and as a textual form. Crapsey argued that even Saintsbury, with his oversimplified view of prosody, recognized "the 'non-coincidence' of verse- and speech-units, particularly . . . of the foot and word," claiming that "his constantly increasing emphasis on just this point of the non-coincidence of foot- and word-division" would ultimately be his most important legacy.[29]

In spite of this crucial advancement, Crapsey argued, no one had yet teased out "the full theoretical implication of the observed fact [of the non-coincidence of foot and word] . . . and there is consequently no generalized theoretical statement of it."[30] This was the necessary next stage, according to Crapsey–a general theory of prosody that would consider both speech units and the prosodical units derived from classical systems as interlocking components of a complex formal whole with many branches and many formal possibilities. She argued that such a theory could come from new methods of metrical analysis–specifically, "a method allowing that close study of the sub-structural arrangement which is necessary to a proper understanding of the co-existent verse-arrangement. Such methodical investigation must . . . begin at the basic point, the relation of the foot to the word."[31]

Crapsey began her application of phonetics to metrical problems by arguing that attending to both syllabic units and metrical units showed that English poetry was made up of "two main rhythms, duple and triple," which could be further subdivided into "duple rhythm, rising and falling, and triple rhythm, rising and falling." She explained in duple rhythms, "the 'normal' syllabic unit, or foot, contains two syllables; in triple rhythm three syllables; the difference in cadence, whether rising or falling, is determined by the position of the 'strong' or 'accented' syllable."[32] The advantage of using the terms duple and triple rhythm, according to Crapsey, was that they were "widely enough used to be generally intelligible without special explanation and their relation to the more frequently used classical terms sufficiently obvious."[33] That is, Crapsey noted, duple rising rhythms were correlated to iambic patterns, duple falling to trochaic patterns, triple rising to anapestic patterns, and triple falling to dactylic patterns.[34] But unlike those classical terms, her terminology placed emphasis on the overall sound effects of poetic lines, which included both syllabic groups and accentual patterns, while the classical terms were apt to confuse students about the units on which poetic rhythms were based.

For Crapsey, developing a less mystified terminology for poetic rhythm–one based on the rhythms of English words rather than on the rhythms of Greek or Latin–was not the only step to advancing prosodical studies. She argued that in addition to being able to identify the predominant rhythm of a poem, critics had also to think about whether the rhythm "operat[ed] in relation to a vocabulary of the mono-disyllabic type, or of the type of medium or of extreme structural complexity."[35] There was, in other words, the linguistic question of how words and feet tended to correlate in different bodies of poetry. Crapsey believed that this consideration further subdivided the possible types of English verse into "six main specialized conditions–(or twelve, allowing for the two varieties in each rhythm."[36]

Though this classificatory system could seem like a footnote in larger prosodical discussions, Crapsey argued that it had major implications for the way critics conducted comparative analyses of different poets. She cited, for instance, a study by John Williams White that posited "a literal technical advance from Milton to Tennyson," and argued that, if my analysis is correct . . . it means that no such advance can exist, at least for the particular poems analyzed, since in them Milton and Tennyson work with reference to differentiated technical problems. Milton deals with the problems that I have indicated as inherent in a vocabulary of extreme structural complexity; his greater variety of word-forms imposes upon him all the difficulties of their manipulation, problems of weighting, of the management of the delicate, and treacherous, secondary accent syllables, and with these, since it is verse in duple rhythm, the question of variant feet. These things if present for Tennyson are far less acutely present and with the change in the basic condition of the vocabulary, the whole weighting and balance of the line change.[37]

Milton and Tennyson were, in essence, working with different materials; comparing them in terms of who was more "advanced" in technique would be akin to comparing a sculptor working in marble and one working in plaster. Crapsey demonstrates here a useful skepticism about progressive accounts of meter as a form that advances or evolves, favoring instead a view that appreciates the multiple possibilities always available to poets working in English. Such a view did not rule out comparative analysis, Crapsey argued, but it did change which poets' techniques could be rightly compared: "The proper comparison, as I make it out, is between Tennyson and Pope," though she noted that "there are between these two poets important secondary differences."[38] Similarly, she argued that comparisons of Swinburne's and Milton's technique had missed the mark because Swinburne's vocabulary was simple and his rhythm triple, while Milton's rhythm was duple. She objected to analyses such as Gilbert Murray's, who argued "that we find in Swinburne a poet using all the resources of the language," when in reality, she believed, "we find in him not a highly developed but an early technique. He has not mastered all the resources of the language; he has not even divined their existence."[39]

Crapsey did still argue for the existence of a perfectible tradition of English poetry, and suggested that her approach to meter could better reveal when a particular type of poetic form had reached its pinnacle. She took Milton and Swinburne as her examples, arguing that if Swinburne indeed stood at "the beginning of a sequence" while Milton had arrived "at the end of a long sequence in development," then it was possible to "suppose we are moving in the great main line of development in English poetry towards a mastery of triple rhythms."[40] In other words, understanding the multiple systems individual poets worked with would allow analysts to "approach, by intelligible stages, a completer understanding of the whole complexity of English verse-structure."[41] Crapsey posited that new methods of study would differentiate twentieth-century from nineteenth-century understandings of prosody, arguing that "our scrutiny will contain within itself a whole series of re-actions which, as felt not at all, or felt in some degree short of complete awareness, did not enter into the making of nineteenth century judgments."[42] Twentieth-century judgments would be derived from "an increase in fully conscious perception" thanks to laboratory experiments.[43] Like her modernist counterparts in linguistics labs all across the country, Crapsey saw twentieth-century science as the key to fully unlocking the mysteries of language that had hitherto kept critics from treating poetic rhythm as nuanced and multiple.

Ironically, in making these claims for the distinctiveness of the discoveries of twentieth-century prosody, Crapsey was repeating a trope of nineteenth-century prosodic discourse—the statement of relief that definitive answers were in sight at last.[44] As Josh King notes, in 1857, Coventry Patmore had claimed, " 'I believe that I am now, for the first time, stating 'the great general law' of meter,'" while thirty years later, Gerard Manley Hopkins wrote, "I believe that I can now set metre and music both of them on a scientific footing which will be final like the law of gravitation."[45] Indeed, a search of the Princeton Prosody Archive, a database of versification manuals, histories of prosody, elocution guides, and related materials, for the term "general law" in texts from the 19th century turns up 704 occurrences of the term in 319 works, while "great law" returns 266 occurrences in 194 works. Part of what makes Crapsey's *Study* difficult reading is the way that she does and does not acknowledge the impossibility of settling the question of how to approach prosody definitively. On the one hand, she recognized the interpretive nature of prosody and the complications with declaring new methods or theories to be definitive, noting midway through her *Study* that "one is of course all the time working 'by ear'–but by a reasoned and tested hearing."[46] If the "reasoned and tested" ear comes from particular kinds of education and training, then of course there is nothing natural to discover about how prosody works, no matter how fine-tuned one's laboratory instruments may become. At the same time, Crapsey appealed to something like an innate sense of rhythm, arguing that although "there is much question" about prosodical terminology, "as to the verse to be identified . . . very little."[47] In other words, though theorists may not agree what to call various kinds of poetic patterns, they also recognize that they empirically existed. The experience of feeling or sensing rhythm here becomes a way for Crapsey to skirt terminological details that point to much deeper divisions within prosodic analysis about the nature of the English language (accentual, syllabic, some combination of the two, or something else altogether).

Another part of what makes *A Study in English Metrics* difficult reading is its lack of a conclusion. Crapsey positions her work as a preliminary investigation that will be useful for other scholars to build on. She provides evidence that the types of vocabulary used by different poets vary, but offers only tables filled with "preliminary data for the closer study of the mono-dissyllabic group hitherto treated as a whole," and instructions that "the closer study of the polysyllable group must be carried out in the same way."[48] Her study ends with tables identifying her findings rather than with a full description of those findings or with an explanation of the broader conclusions she draws from the specific analyses. Mary Elizabeth Osborn sought to apply Crapsey's analytical methods to Crapsey's own poetry in 1928, concluding that "Crapsey's vocabulary falls easily into type II, the type of medium structural complexity,"[49] but beyond that few critics have attempted to extrapolate theories from Crapsey's preliminary study. What might Crapsey's poetry tell us about her vision of prosodical analysis?

In Crapsey's syllabic poetry, we see her experimenting with the interplay of poetic patterns that are heard, seen, felt, and implied–an interplay that never settles down into a singular pattern, but that keeps multiple options in play simultaneously. Take, for instance, "The Sun-Dial," which reads in its entirety:

> Every day,
> Every day,
> Tell the hours
> By their shadows,
> By their shadows.[50]

   This can be read as a syllabic form with lines of 3, 3, 3, 4, and 4 syllables, or with lines of 3, 3, 4, 4, and 4 syllables, or a syllabic form with five lines of four syllables each, or various combinations of those patterns, depending on whether "every" is pronounced with two or three syllables and whether "hours" is one or two syllables. Crapsey defines a polysyllable as a word over two syllables in length, but doesn't give guidelines for determining how to count syllables. What we do know of her reading practices does not help those guidelines to materialize, as she evinced an interest in sounds apart from sense.[51] Is the piece emphasizing the length of an hour, the way that time can drag, and hence stretching "ev-er-y" across the length of three syllables, or contrasting the beat of the short "ev-ry days" with the lengthening shadows in the lines of 4 syllables? Thinking about syllables in relation to feet also doesn't settle the question, as the lines of 4 are trochaic but the variable lines don't have a clear relation to the trochee.
   The possible foot combinations hinge on these questions of pronunciation. The poem could be scanned:

/ x /		/ x x /
Eve ry day,	OR	Ev er y day,
/ x /		
Eve ry day,		
/ x /		/ x / x
Tell the hours	OR	Tell the hours

```
/   x  /   x
By their shadows,
/   x   /   x
By their shadows.
```

If "Every day" is a three-syllable line, it's either a cretic foot (stress, unstress, stress) or a trochee with an extra syllable. If it's a four-syllable line, it's a trochee followed by an iamb. If "hours" is stretched across four syllables, the line is trochaic, like the final two lines, but if it's compressed into a single syllable, it would follow the pattern of the compressed pronunciation of "every day." In a poem about measuring time, we can hear both the steady tick of a clock (4/4/4/4/4) and the lengthening shadows registered by the sun dial (3/3/3/4/4). The immaterial—time, shadows—is materialized in the count, even as the count itself remains composed of shadow syllables. Rather than deciding on a definitive experience of time or a definitive mode of measuring, the poem registers multiple temporal counts, displaying the idea of the multiplicity within prosody. What does it mean to measure time through language in a language without syllabic quantity? The question remains.

Crapsey's cinquains tend to be more reliably iambic than "The Sun-Dial," but even here, counting remains a fraught endeavor. Take the poem "Triad":

> These be
> Three silent things:
> The falling snow . . . the hour
> Before the dawn . . . the mouth of one
> Just dead.[52]

Much like the funny math in Wordsworth's "We Are Seven," counting in "Triad" is complicated by the endeavor to represent absence textually and aurally. The "three silent things" are spread out over the line breaks so that graphically they look like five things ("the falling snow," "the hour," "before the dawn," "the mouth of one," "just dead"). The silent things are spoken in iambic, or rising (to use Crapsey's terminology) lines, but can also be read as beginning and ending with spondees, or "loud" accents (if we take accent to be equated with vocal emphasis). The ellipses in the lines counting the silent things likewise point to present absences, hovering at a sonic level below an unstressed syllable but as equally present to the eye as any of the sounded syllables in the text. Measuring may be meant to clarify and explain, the poem seems to suggest, but measuring syllables proves to be harder than simply counting. How does one measure the difference between a graphic silence (...) and an audible silence? How does one count absence? What happens when the eye and the ear don't count the same things?

I want to close by suggesting that the present absences in Crapsey's count provide a way to understand the figure of Crapsey's ailing body within scholarship about her work. The image of the dying woman laboring against a relentless countdown necessarily remains a part of her legacy, and part of our accounting for her work. But like the suspended questions about accent and syllable breaks within her lines, that figure does and does not resolve questions about her poetry and her metrical theories. While we may see and hear the pathos of a woman representing her own death through the play of shadowy syllables and unreliable methods of measuring time, presence, and absence, we also have to make sure that we are accounting for the woman still finding her place in the realm of the living. By consciously responding to Bridges and Saintsbury and seeking out other scholars to read and comment on her work, Crapsey showed herself to be deeply engaged in scholarly conversations about prosody. Her legacy is both the tragic beauty of her poetry and the engagement with contemporaneous prosodic discourse within its lines. The lesson her work teaches us is perhaps the value of keeping interpretive questions about prosody suspended, partway between answers that never firmly settle into a final form.

NOTES

1 Llewellyn Jones, "Adelaide Crapsey: Poet and Critic," *The North American Review* 217, no. 809 (April 1923): 539.

2 Karen Alkalay-Gut, "The Dying of Adelaide Crapsey," *Journal of Modern Literature* 13, no. 2 (1986): 225, 228.

3 That Crapsey was interested in contemporary conversations about prosody is well documented. Crapsey wrote to the respected scholar of prosody T.S. Omond asking for feedback on her work, and she sought out Cornell professor Martin Sampson, a Milton scholar, for further conversations about prosody and composition. Karen Alkalay-Gut, *Alone in the Dawn: The Life of Adelaide Crapsey* (Athens, GA: University of Georgia Press, 1988), 233, 241.

4 For an overview of the field of historical poetics, see Yopie Prins, "What is Historical Poetics?" *Modern Language Quarterly* 77, no. 1 (2016): 13-40. Field-defining works include Prins's "Victorian Meters," in *The Cambridge Companion to Victorian Poetry*, ed. Joseph Bristow (Cambridge: Cambridge University Press, 2000), 89-113; Virginia Jackson, *Dickinson's Misery* (Princeton: Princeton University Press, 2005); Meredith McGill, ed., *The Traffic in Poems: Nineteenth-Century Poetry and Transatlantic Exchange* (Rutgers University Press, 2008); Jason Hall, ed., *Meter Matters: Verse Cultures of the Long Nineteenth Century* (Columbus: Ohio University Press, 2011).

5 Meredith Martin, *The Rise and Fall of Meter: Poetry and English National Culture, 1860-1930* (Princeton: Princeton University Press, 2012), 2, 18.

6 Ibid., 204.

7 Ibid., 40.

8 Ibid., 35.

9 For more on the intensification of laboratory-based investigations of poetic rhythm at the end of the nineteenth century, see Jason David Hall, *Nineteenth-Century Verse and Technology: Machines of Meter* (Palgrave Macmillan, 2017) and "Materializing Meter: Physiology, Psychology, Prosody," *Victorian Poetry* 49, no. 2 (2011): 179-197, as well as Michael Golston, *Rhythm and Race in Modernist Poetry and Science* (Columbia University Press, 2007).

10 Amy Lowell, "The Rhythms of Free Verse," *The Dial* 64, no. 758 (Jan. 1918): 51, 54-55.

11 Ibid., 56.

12 Martin, *Rise and Fall*, 88.

13 Ibid., 89.

14 Ibid., 96.

15 Ibid., 97-98.

16 Adelaide Crapsey, *A Study in English Metrics* (New York: Knopf, 1918), 32.

17 Ibid., 69.

18 Ibid., 30.

19 Ibid.

20 For more on Crapsey and modernist syllabics, see Meredith Martin, "Picturing Rhythm," in *Critical Rhythm*, ed. Jonathan Culler and Benjamin Glaser, forthcoming from Fordham University Press.

21 Crapsey, *A Study*, 33.

22 Golston, *Rhythm and Race*, 3.

23 Crapsey, *A Study*, 33.

24 Ibid., 32.

25 Ibid., 34.

26 Ibid., 36.

27 Ibid., 37.

28 Ibid., 38.

29 Ibid., 39.

30 Ibid., 40-41.

31 Ibid., 44.

32 Ibid., 51

33 Ibid.

34 Ibid., 52.

35 Ibid., 53.

36 Ibid.

37 Ibid., 62-63.

38 Ibid., 63.

39 Ibid., 68.

40 Ibid., 68-69.

41 Ibid., 74.

42 Ibid., 69.

43 Ibid.

44 Martin notes that such tropes were crucial parts of nineteenth-century approaches to prosody, and that "common tropes of the prosodic handbook" included "new marking systems, new names for metrical feet, and new definitions of and arguments over the definitions of terms." These multiplying systems and methodological disagreements "created the field of prosody" as prosodists "account[e]d for each other's theories . . . and [put] forth their corrections, adjustments, and improvements, both of each other and, in a series of revised and reprinted editions, of themselves." Martin, *Rise and Fall*, 45.

45 Joshua King, "Patmore, Hopkins, and the Problem of the English Metrical Law," *Victorian Poetry* 49, no. 2 (2011): 31.

46 Crapsey, *A Study*, 45.

47 Ibid., 52.

48 Ibid., 74.

49 Mary Elizabeth Osborn, "The Vocabulary in Adelaide Crapsey's Verse," *American Speech* 3, no. 6 (1928): 459.

50 Adelaide Crapsey, *Verse* (New York: Knopf, 1922), 69.

51 According to a friend of Crapsey's, it was the vowel sounds in "Lycidas" that had led to her passion for prosody: "She felt that certain combinations of sound were particularly effective, and she had tried for these combinations in a poem which she had just finished. She read it aloud, and then the vowel sounds alone to show the sequence of rising and falling tones." Osborn qtd. in Alkalay-Gut, "The Dying," 231. This was apparently a frequent practice, as another source notes that Crapsey also read her poem "Song" as "an exercise in vowel sequence" by "dropping the consonants altogether and leaving it as a series of vowel sounds only." Loescher qtd. in Alkalay-Gut, "The Dying," 231n9.

52 Crapsey, *Verse*, 33.

COPYING CHARMS: ADELAIDE CRAPSEY'S DEBT TO CHEROKEE INCANTATIONS

Rose Gubele

ROSE GUBELE is the director of first-year composition at the University of Central Missouri where she teaches courses in rhetoric and writing. Her research focuses on Native American rhetorics, racism, and Cherokee rhetorics.

Adelaide Crapsey's life was brief, tragic, and mysterious. It is human nature to speculate when confronted with a mystery, and speculation concerning Crapsey's invention of the cinquain is extensive. As Susan Sutton Smith states in her book, *Complete Poems and Collected Letters of Adelaide Crapsey*, the form of the cinquain has been misunderstood. As Smith argues, "The relation of the cinquain to Japanese forms . . . has long been disputed."[1] Though most scholars suggest that the cinquain was inspired by Japanese poetic forms haiku and tanka, some have stated that the cinquain was purely Crapsey's invention. Some have even argued that Crapsey had no knowledge of tanka poetry when she created the cinquain.[2] That assertion was later proved false when a manuscript of tanka poetry was found in Crapsey's papers. It is clear that the cinquain was influenced by Japanese forms; however, the exact nature and extent of the influence is still unclear.[3]

Scholars have assumed that the cinquain was heavily influenced by Japanese poetic forms. Despite this, another potential source of inspiration has been overlooked. While she was in preparatory school at Kemper Hall in Kenosha, Wisconsin, Crapsey studied Cherokee incantations which were published by James Mooney, a noted anthropologist who worked with the Eastern Cherokee Nation.[4] Most scholars don't connect Crapsey's work with these Cherokee forms, but in Susan Sutton Smith's dissertation, which was later revised and published as the *Complete Poems and Collected Letters of Adelaide Crapsey,* a brief link was established. However, Smith's discussion of Cherokee incantations was omitted from the published edition. Biographer Karen Alkalay-Gut also acknowledges Crapsey's work with Cherokee incantations, but diminishes their importance. She claims that concerning Crapsey's work with Cherokee incantations, "little is known, except the fact of their existence" and that "They seem to be exercises in sounds and oral patterns."[5] The only other comment Alkalay-Gut has concerning Crapsey's work with Cherokee forms is that the work may have led to her "laughable approach to spelling," although she also says "A learning disability might also have been the cause."[6] The prejudice in Alkalay-Gut's words is clear. This bias has caused Alkalay-Gut and others to dismiss Crapsey's work with Cherokee forms as a curiosity of little consequence. Nonetheless, the similarities between Crapsey's cinquains and Cherokee incantations suggest a much greater influence.

The incantations that Crapsey studied are used in Cherokee healing rituals by medicine men and women. Before the introduction of the Cherokee syllabary, these incantations were memorized. However, in 1821, Sequoyah (George Guess) invented an 86-character syllabary which represented sounds in the Cherokee language, a syllable-based system which enabled Cherokee speakers to write their own language. After Sequoyah's invention, Cherokee healers began writing down their incantations in the syllabary.[7] These incantations were kept in "medicine books," small ledger books, or were written down on any available scrap of paper.[8] The incantations of Cherokee medicine people first came to be acknowledged by non-Cherokees when anthropologist James Mooney collected approximately six hundred samples written in the Sequoyah syllabary from the Eastern Cherokee in 1887 and 1888. Mooney called these incantations "sacred formulas," [9] and published the texts (written phonetically, in accented Latin characters) with English translations and commentary. Mooney's informer, a Cherokee medicine man named *Ayuini*, or "Swimmer," provided him with the bulk of this collection.[10] It is Mooney's manuscript that Crapsey studied.

Mooney transcribed texts that Swimmer provided him, translated them, and explained their significance. In his text, he copies the incantations in prose form. Cherokee scholars Jack Frederick and Anna Gritts Kilpatrick state that Mooney "does violence" to the structure of the incantations he references because they should be written with line breaks, like traditional poetry.[11] Though Mooney's method is not optimal, the poetic beauty of the incantations is still apparent in his text. Cherokee incantations, as they are intended to be spoken or written, feature shorter lines, meant to indicate voice breaks when the medicine person speaks the incantations over their patients. They look like poetry. In fact, Jack Frederick Kilpatrick has argued that they are literature.[12] Crapsey, like Kilpatrick, saw the beauty of Cherokee incantations. She transcribed sections from Mooney's *Sacred Formulas*, then rearranged incantations with line breaks so that they looked like traditional poetry. She studied the forms, and was inspired by them; the evidence of this exists in her cinquains, some of which contain elements from Cherokee incantations. However, it is unlikely that Crapsey understood the significance of the elements of the incantations. Mooney didn't explain the incantations' forms or patterns in his work. Even so, many elements are observable upon careful study of the pieces.

Cherokee incantations typically follow a few patterns which create a ceremonial aura. It must be noted that not all of these elements are present in every incantation; however, the features listed are common mechanisms used in many incantations. The incantations usually begin with an attention-getting word or phrase, often *Gha!* or *Sge!* (Now! or Listen!). This opening serves to "awaken" the spirits so that the medicine person is certain to have their attention.[13]

Incantations can also contain a variety of verbal forms which make them very tricky to translate. For example, they include loanwords from other tribes:

> Manuscript works on medicine and magic among the Oklahoma Cherokees sometimes contain . . . texts of charm songs that, although written or partially written in the Sequoyah syllabary, are not in the Cherokee language. Cherokee din(a) da:hnvwi:sg(i) (those who cure them=medicine men), who, as a rule, know no Indian language other than their own, are aware that such writings, in some instances handed down to them through several generations, are in either Creek or Natchez. But only rarely does one encounter a medicine man who thinks that he knows the meaning of a specific word here or there. More commonly, he will not even know the general drift of what is written and is not quite sure which particular grouping of syllables constitutes a word. But he does know that his saying or song is powerful—"alive," as he expresses it—and there the matter rests.[14]

Incantations contain ancient forms of Cherokee, and words that have no known definition. All of these difficult to translate elements in incantations make them, what Alan Kilpatrick calls, a form of "cryptography."[15] The loanwords, archaic words, and undefinable words help to create texts that are nearly written in code and are difficult to translate by anyone who is not a Cherokee medicine person.[16] Incantations are also filled with ritualistic phrases; for example, the phrase "Long Person" is often used to refer to water (river).[17] Occasionally, references to Jesus Christ, the Trinity, and other Christian references also appear in incantations.[18] [19]

Another element of incantations is that they contain "identity tags," usually statements such as "this is my name" and "these are my people," which designate the particular name and clan affiliation of the client.[20] A spirit is also petitioned by name for magical aid, and a ritual color is identified which suggests the spirit's magical role. The location of the spirit's residence is named, and the spirit's limitless power is acknowledged.[21] In Cherokee spirituality, colors are associated with qualities, and most are associated with compass directions as well:

> Red—East—Victory, power.
> Blue—North—Failure, weakness, spiritual depression.
> Black—West—Death, oblivion.
> White—South—Happiness, peace.
> Brown—Normality, the earth.
> Purple—Witchcraft, evil.
> Yellow—A sinister influence, or power.[22] [23]

The symbolic associations of the colors are invoked in their ritual use in incantation. In addition to the inclusion of color symbolism, incantations also frequently make use of two numbers that are sacred to Cherokees, the numbers four and, most sacred of all, seven. Often, an important word will be repeated four or seven times during a ritual. A line may also be repeated four or seven times, and in some cases, the numbers themselves are named in the incantation.[24]

Incantations also typically use a special verb suffix,[25] -iga-, which is not typically used in everyday speech. The verb is an "immediate past tense," and it means that "at the time of speaking, the action has just been performed."[26] The use of this verb is significant because it appears often in Cherokee incantations as a "time-conflating device" that "specifies the immediacy of one's actions in the context of time."[27] As Alan Kilpatrick explains:

> To illustrate this dynamic consider the phrase "I have just come to draw away your soul." Whereas, the phrase, "I have come to draw away your soul," would simply announce one's intention, the shamanistic insertion of the adverb *just* dramatizes the fact that this ritualistic moment is now being actualized by the speaker's presence.

Just is a qualifying adverb that specifies the immediacy of one's actions in the context of time (e.g., "I have just been there" or "I have just been told"). By declaring their intention (e.g., to draw away the victim's soul) as a semi-completed temporal action reciters reinforce the illusion that metamorphosis has actually set in, that reality has already("just now") been transcended.[28] The use of *-iga-* helps to create a sense of immediacy. The action is about to happen and has already happened.

Because incantations are created by many different medicine men and women with varying styles, there is a great deal of diversity. However, according to Jack Frederick and Anna Gritts Kilpatrick, a *characteristic* incantation would look something like this:

> Now! Listen!
> Red Raven!
> Your Place of Peace is Above.
> You are a Great Wizard.
> You fail in nothing.
> Quickly You have just come to hear.[29]

In the above example, Raven is the spirit petitioned. In traditional Cherokee stories, Raven is an important spirit. There was a time when there was no fire, and the Thunders (also spirits) had the only fire that had come from their lightning. They kept this fire in a hollow sycamore and kept it from the rest of the world. In this story, Raven was the first spirit to try to get the fire and bring it to warm the rest of the animals. Although Raven was ultimately unable to get the fire, the fire scorched his feathers while he tried, which explains why ravens are black.[30] Because of this story, ravens are linked to fire, which is sacred to Cherokees. Raven has literally been purified by fire, so he often appears in incantations. The color, Red is also used, and Red is associated with victory.

It is unclear how much of Mooney's work Crapsey read, but the fact that she recopied sections from his *Sacred Formulas of the Cherokees* suggests that the work captivated her. Crapsey's cinquains contain patterns that exist in Cherokee incantations. In the Cinquain "November Night," for example, Crapsey begins the way virtually all Cherokee incantations begin, with an imperative, using the term "listen":

> Listen. .
> With faint dry sound,
> Like stops of passing ghosts,
> The leaves, frost-crisp'd, break from the trees
> And fall.[31]

Similarly, in "Snow," she begins with the imperative "Look up":

> Look up . . .
> From bleakening hills
> Blows down the light, first breath
> Of wintry wind . . . look up, and scent
> The Snow![32]

Even when Crapsey does not use imperatives, the state invoked by their use is evident in her poems. According to Susan Sutton Smith, "these imperatives command or announce expectancy or waiting, an attitude or gesture common to many Crapsey poems."[33]

Crapsey also uses the immediate past tense in some of her cinquains, a construction that is essential to Cherokee incantations. In "The Warning," Crapsey begins with this construction, indicating that the white moth flew "just now," suggesting the sense of immediacy:

> Just now,
> Out of the strange
> Still dusk . . . as strange, as still . . .
> A white moth flew. Why am I grown
> So cold?[34]

Crapsey also includes a Cherokee cultural reference in the cinquain, "Winter." In the poem she writes:

> The cold
> With steely clutch
> Grips all the land . . . alack,
> The little people in the hills
> Will die![35]

The "Little People" she mentions are likely to be Cherokee Little People, Yûñwĭ Tsunsdi', whom Mooney identifies as spirit beings. Similar to Celtic Faeries, Little People live in the hills and are known to be magical beings who enjoy playing tricks on humans.[36]

Despite the one reference to Little People, most of the Cherokee cultural context was unavailable to her. Smith points out that "much, perhaps too much, is lost in translation."[37] The same is true of Crapsey's examination of Japanese forms, raising questions of appropriation. Crapsey did copy the forms of Cherokee incantations and is never recorded as giving them credit as an influence on her work. She did the same with Japanese forms. Nonetheless, it is difficult to view Crapsey's careful examination of Cherokee incantations as unethical. She saw value in the incantations when they went largely ignored by non-Cherokees. She also studied the forms carefully and noticed patterns, a fact that suggests her admiration of the incantations. Crapsey appeared to view them as pieces of literature, and with good reason. Native scholars may have differing views on whether or not Crapsey appropriated Native forms, but one Cherokee scholar seemed to want non-Indians to view and appreciate Cherokee incantations. Jack Frederick Kilpatrick writes:

> Recently I read in the Encyclopedia Britannica that no native American society north of Mexico had produced a literature; yet during the past five years alone I have collected from attics, barns, caves, and jars buried in the ground some ten thousand poetical texts, many of which would excite the envy of a Hafiz or Li Tai Po.[39]

Kilpatrick considers the incantations to be more than spiritual documents; to him, they are literary works. He sees them as gifts to share with the world. Crapsey did place value in Japanese and Cherokee forms. Thus, it is likely that her creation of the cinquain, and much of her poetry, was influenced by both.

NOTES

1   Susan Sutton Smith, *Complete Poems and Collected Letters of Adelaide Crapsey.* (New York: SUNY Press, 1977), 25.

2   Mary Edwardine O'Connor, "Adelaide Crapsey: A Biographical Study." (master's thesis, University of Notre Dame, 1913), 26.

3   Ibid., 25-26

4   Karen Alkalay-Gut, *Alone in the Dawn: The Life of Adelaide Crapsey*, (Athens: University of Georgia Press, 2008), 337 n56; Susan Sutton Smith, *Complete Poems and Collected Letters of Adelaide Crapsey*, 142.

5   Karen Alkalay-Gut, *Alone in the Dawn*, 337 n56.

6   Ibid., 59.

7   John Witthoft, *Green Corn Ceremonialism in the Eastern Woodlands.* (Ann Arbor: University of Michigan Press, 1949), 36n.

8   Jack Frederick and Anna Gritts Kilpatrick, *Run Toward the Nightland: Magic of the Oklahoma Cherokees*, (Dallas: Southern Methodist University Press, 1967), 3.

9   The term "incantations" is used throughout instead of Mooney's term, "sacred formulas," because Mooney's term is not accurate. Incantations are not formulaic, and not all are sacred; some are utilitarian or designed to harm. The Kilpatricks use the Cherokee term *igawesdi*, which means "to say, one" (The term incantation is closer to the Cherokee word Mooney's term, so it will be used throughout [see Jack Frederick and Anna Gritts Kilpatrick, *Walk in Your Soul: Love Incantations of the Oklahoma Cherokees*, (Dallas: Southern Methodist University Press, 1965), 4; Jack Frederick and Anna Gritts Kilpatrick, *Run Toward the Nightland*, 6].

10 James Mooney, *James Mooney's History, Myths, and Sacred Formulas of the Cherokees.* (Fairview, NC: Historical Images, 1992), 307 and 311.

11 Jack Frederick and Anna Gritts Kilpatrick, *Walk in Your Soul*, 7.

12 Jack Frederick Kilpatrick, "The Buckskin Curtain," *Southwest Review* 52, no. 1 (1967): 83-87, 85.

13 Alan Kilpatrick, *The Night has a Naked Soul: Witchcraft and Sorcery Among the Western Cherokee*, (Syracuse University Press, 1997), 30.

14 Jack Frederick and Anna Gritts Kilpatrick, *Muskogean Charm Songs Among the Oklahoma Cherokees*, (Smithsonian Contributions to Anthropology. 2.3 Washington: Smithsonian, 1967), 29.

15 Alan Kilpatrick, *The Night has a Naked Soul*, 36).

16 Though, as stated above, it is often difficult even for a Cherokee medicine person to translate parts of these texts.

17 Alan Kilpatrick, *The Night has a Naked Soul*, 39.

18 Cherokee medicine people see no inconsistency in mixing Christian symbolism and what many Christians would call "pagan" spirituality. In fact, it is reported that "all of today's conjurors consider themselves to be good Christians and feel

that their work is completely consistent with Christian doctrine," Raymond D. Fogelson, "Change, Persistence, and Accommodation in Cherokee Medico-Magical Beliefs, No 21," *Symposium on Cherokee and Iroquois Culture*. eds. William N. Fenton and John Glick (Washington, DC: US Government Printing Office, Smithsonian Institution, Bureau of American Ethnology, Bulletin 180, 1961).

19 Jack Frederick Kilpatrick, "Christian Motifs in Cherokee Healing Rituals," *The Perkins School of Theology Journal* 18, no. 2 (1965): 33-36, 34.

20 Alan Kilpatrick, *The Night has a Naked Soul*, 29.

21 Jack Frederick and Anna Gritts Kilpatrick, *Walk in Your Soul*, 6.

22 Ibid., 8.

23 James Mooney has a slightly different view of the sacred colors. He includes only six, omitting purple, and though he has similar interpretations of many of the colors, he tries to ascribe directions to all of them (my guess is that in his Eurocentric mindset, he wanted to have consistency). I'm using the Kilpatricks' version of the sacred colors, because it is more accurate than Mooney's version [see James Mooney, *James Mooney's History, Myths, and Sacred Formulas of the Cherokees*. (Fairview, NC: Historical Images, 1992), 342].

24 Jack Frederick and Anna Gritts Kilpatrick, *Walk in Your Soul: Love Incantations of the Oklahoma Cherokees*, (Dallas: Southern Methodist University Press, 1965), 5.

25 Cherokee verbs are extremely complex. There are over 100,000 forms of each verb [see Jack Frederick Kilpatrick, "Verbs are Kings at Panther Place: The Cherokee Tongue Verses 'English,'" *Southwest Review* 50, no. 4 (1965): 372-376, 372].

26 Jack Frederick and Anna Gritts Kilpatrick, *New Echota Letters: Contributions of Samuel A. Worcester to the Cherokee Phoenix*, (Dallas: Southern Methodist University Press, 1968), 67.

27 Alan Kilpatrick, *The Night has a Naked Soul*, 32.

28 Ibid., 32, emphasis his.

29 Ibid., 6.

30 James Mooney, *James Mooney's History, Myths, and Sacred Formulas of the Cherokees*, 240-241.

31 Adelaide Crapsey, *Verse*, (New York: Alfred A. Knopf, 1922), 31.

32 Ibid., 34.

33 Susan Sutton Smith, *Complete Poems and Collected Letters of Adelaide Crapsey*, 36.

34 Ibid., 49.

35 Ibid., 41.

36 James Mooney, *James Mooney's History, Myths, and Sacred Formulas of the Cherokees*, 333.

37 Susan Sutton Smith, "The Poems of Adelaide Crapsey: A Critical Edition with an Introduction and Notes" (dissertation, University of Rochester, 1972), cxii.

38 Jack Frederick Kilpatrick, "The Buckskin Curtain," 85.

"FROST-CRISP'D" VERSES: ADELAIDE CRAPSEY'S CINQUAINS AND THE POETICS OF ILLNESS

Patrick Thomas Henry

PATRICK THOMAS HENRY is the Associate Editor for Fiction and Poetry at Modern Language Studies. *His work has appeared in or is forthcoming from* Fiction Southeast, Passages North, *and* Massachusetts Review, *amongst other publications. He currently teaches creative writing at the University of North Dakota.*

> If illness' end be health regained then I
> Will pay you, Asculapeus, when I die.
> – Adelaide Crapsey, "Epigram"

1.

In a February 1914 letter to her friend Esther Lowenthal, Adelaide Crapsey reports from Saranac Lake on a treatment for her collapsed lung. The cause of her respiratory complaints is tuberculosis, which would take Crapsey's life in October of that year. "I had hoped to have the 'notes' ready by this time," Crapsey comments, in reference to *A Study in English Metrics* (1915), "but my mild prosodic fit was interrupted by the pneumo thorax treatment. Yes its [sic] the treatment you speak of—the lung is collapsed—therefore gets an absolute rest."[1] She attempts to deflect attention away from her pain by parroting some clinical language about the treatment's "60% success rate." However, this treatment is immensely painful: it requires physicians to puncture a patient's collapsed lung with a needle before using a gas to re-inflate it. Yet, Crapsey pivots from an imitation of surgical chatter to the whimsy of a comedy of manners:

> Dr Baldwin tried 3 places and struck each time in [an] adhesion (inner and outer lining of something stuck together) so that the gas wouldnt [sic] go in. They worked a little over an hour and by that time we were all tired so we gave it up and now we[']ll try again. It isn't awfully bad you know though not what one would choose for a diversion.[2]

Crapsey's glib tone functions like a feint, seeking to distract Lowenthal from the suffering associated with tuberculosis.[3] But it also minimizes another, equally problematic reading of the poet and her work: the romantic conflation of illness and artistry. Crapsey is not the "patient etherised on the table," to which T.S. Eliot likens the brooding J. Alfred Prufrock.[4] Nor is she the inspirational (if not fetishistic) object of Charles Baudelaire's poem "La Muse Malade" ("The Sick Muse"), in which the subject of disease sparks the speaker's poetic vision. Indeed, it would not be difficult to read Crapsey through this prism—and it's an error that many of her admirers have succumbed to. In a commemoration for the *Vassar Miscellany*, later reprinted in the 1922 edition of Crapsey's *Verse*, Crapsey's friend and Vassar classmate Jean Webster offers this take: "Adelaide Crapsey, by nature as vivid and joyous and alive a spirit as ever loved the beauty of life, like Keats and Stevenson, worked doggedly for many years against the numbing weight of a creeping pitiless disease."[5]

Like the Romantic poet John Keats, Crapsey traveled Europe—even forming a special attachment to Rome—in an effort to mitigate the symptoms of her disease, and yet (like Keats, again) her career as a poet was tragically curtailed by tuberculosis. Furthermore, like the Victorian novelist Robert Louis Stevenson, she viewed travel as a means of acting against the constraints imposed by tuberculosis, and both writers had spent time convalescing at Saranac Lake, New York. Moreover, because of her somewhat cloistered life (she is the mannered daughter of an Episcopal minister), there is the temptation to read in Crapsey the same swell of passion that falsely characterizes other tubercular writers, like Keats or Stevenson. Yet, the treatment of these tubercular writers is markedly gendered: while readers and critics cast Keats and Stevenson's suffering as a heroic striving, Crapsey's earliest eulogists and reviewers read her poems as echoes of the cloistered desires of domestic fiction, akin to the latent yearnings of an Austenian socialite in a sitting room.

Still, the well-intentioned conflation of tuberculosis and passion neglects the pain that Crapsey had experienced from treatments like the pneumothorax punctures and tuberculosis itself. As Susan Sontag reminds us, literary treatments of tuberculosis aptly recognize the disease's association with the lungs, but neglect its effects on the body: *mycobacterium tuberculosis*, the bacteria that causes the illness, leads to chronic fatigue and pain, a wracking cough, fevers, the projection of blood-filled sputum, collapsed lungs, and the deterioration of the lung tissue. Romanticizing her tuberculosis as an artistic disease commits another injustice against Crapsey's legacy: it shutters other ways of reading her creative process. Like the literary experiments of such contemporaries as Virginia Woolf, Crapsey's invention of the cinquain, a short-form poem, mimics the physical and mental impositions of her ill health. Webster's note in the *Vassar Miscellany* reminds the reader that Crapsey devised the form during her illness, and that "[i]t is an example of extremest compression," in that it "reduces an idea to its very lowest terms—and presents it in a single sharp impression."[6] The cinquain allows for the sickbed's fleeting yet intense meditations. Its metrical pattern and enjambment—five compact lines of iambic feet (that is, a foot consisting of an unstressed followed by a stressed syllable)—cause the reader to experience the tubercular patient's seizing of the lungs and jagged breathing alongside sharp, quickened mental labor.

In her letter to Lowenthal, Crapsey situates herself as a writer on the verge of something, albeit a something interrupted, forestalled, and nuanced by her disease. As a poetic form, the cinquain is the manifestation of this creative process, of writing with and against disease. More than anything, the cinquain leaves its readers on the threshold of self-awareness, somewhere between illness and health, between death and life. To explore this in the cinquain, we must complicate previous discussions of Crapsey's biography and her poetic influences, and then situate the cinquain alongside literary Modernism's interest in transforming readers' perspectives.

2.

In her introduction to *The Complete Poems and Collected Letters of Adelaide Crapsey* (1977), Susan Sutton Smith understates critics' tendency to romanticize Crapsey's tuberculosis: "Criticism of Crapsey's poetry suffers from the fondness some admirers have for examining the poems as 'human documents,' which substitutes inaccurate and sentimental thoughts about her life for any consideration of her work."[7] In his foreword to *Verse*, Claude Bragdon establishes this trend by reading Crapsey's illness as if it were the mantle of a gothic heroine:

> I see again her drooping figure with some trail of gossamer bewitchment clinging about or drifting after her. Although her body spoke of a fastidious and sedulous care in keeping with her essentially aristocratic nature, she was merciless in the demands she made upon it, and this was the direct cause

of her loss of health. The keen and shining blade of her spirit too greatly scorned its scabbard the body, and for this she paid the utmost penalty.[8]

Virginia Woolf parodying Ann Radcliffe or Walter Scott could not have better sentimentalized Crapsey's illness: Bragdon reduces her to a trope, the damsel whose every act is redolent of her moral character, class consciousness, and poetic sensibility. However, readers of *Verse* would have encountered poems that speak not to a lily-wilting of the soul, but of a prosody that resists Bragdon's insistence on portraying Crapsey as a modern-day Clarissa—ailing, prim, virginal. Crapsey's cinquains subvert this idealism through contradictions that merge the body and mind, sickness and health, and dark and light. In "Shadow," Crapsey immediately contradicts the title's darkness with a grammatical fragment—"A-sway, / On red rose, / A golden butterfly. ."—but the poem's speaker then internalizes and darkens that image, stating, "And on my heart a butterfly / Night-wing'd."[9] Conventional images of pastoral and poetic pleasure, the red rose and the butterfly of "Shadow" instead become a site of melancholy and unrest. The poem jolts the reader with a frisson of mortal dread through Crapsey's inventive verb "night-wing'd," which—amplified by the enjambment of the final lines—re-stages the rose and the butterfly as harbingers, or perhaps intimations, of death.

Despite the substance of Crapsey's poems, the earlier reviewers of *Verse* were likely swayed by Bragdon's introductory note, which appeared in both the 1915 Manas Press edition and the 1922 Knopf edition. Here is a sampling of book reviews of the 1915 edition, which cement some of those "inaccurate and sentimental thoughts," as Smith might put it.[10] "W.S.B.," the *Boston Transcript*'s reviewer, extols *Verse* as "something too bright to be earthly, something too strong to be mortal." By implication, the anonymous reviewer for a "Book of the Week" feature echoes Webster's conflation of Crapsey's death with Keats: "Claude Bragdon . . . introduces to the English reading world a poet who may worthily join that company who have been snatched untimely from their work by death." In the 1940s, Yvor Winters used similar language when dubbing Crapsey an "immortal poet."[11] Even a 2004 article in *Ars Medica*, entitled "Tuberculosis as Muse," suggests that tuberculosis was responsible for spurring Crapsey to "the expressiveness of poetry" as an articulation of the "inexpressible."[12]

By crafting this angelic and immortal Crapsey, Bragdon has imposed a particular (and totalitarian) understanding of the intersections of illness, authorship, and poetics. Worse yet, this presentation of Crapsey commits an error that Susan Sontag decries in *Illness and Its Metaphors* (1978), namely, that tuberculosis serves as a metaphor for the hidden creative and critical ambitions that "consumed" Crapsey as a poet and a scholar of metrical patterns in English prosody. This scholarly attachment to a figurative Crapsey forecloses a key avenue of inquiry: that is, the manner in which Crapsey, like such contemporaries as Virginia Woolf, devises a creative praxis that seeks to produce empathy with, as opposed to pity for, the ill.

3.

In mining Crapsey's investment in the intersections of illness and poetics, we inherently risk running afoul of Sontag's concerns with the metaphorical overvaluation of disease in literature. Worse yet, there is a Freudian hazard to contend with: a symbolic reading of illness as the manifestation of an artistic spirit. Before Sontag and disability studies offered a corrective, discussions of literature and medicine often followed the tack of Edmund Wilson or Lionel Trilling. In "Philoctetes: The Wound and the Bow," Wilson reads the snake-bitten Greek hero Philoctetes as evidence of "the conception of superior strength as inseparable from disability"[13]—that is, an example of what Robert McRuer and other disability studies scholars might identify as the "supercrip" stereotype. Trilling's take on illness and creativity is not dissimilar. "As for the artist," Trilling says, in a gloss of

Freud, "he is virtually in the same category with the neurotic."[14] Elsewhere, Trilling suggests that the romanticized "myth of the sick artist is the institutional sanction" of "sensitive people," who themselves wish to lay claim to the artist's mantle.[15]

Conceptually, Wilson and Trilling are simply presenting the same fallacy as Crapsey's early critics, albeit in more scholarly trappings. Their authoritative voices also misconstrue how Crapsey's contemporaries spoke of disease and the artistic temperament. For instance, William James in *The Principles of Psychology* (1890) writes of the "paramount reality of sensation" and concludes that "tangibles [like pain or pleasure] . . . concern us most; and the other senses, so far as their practical use goes, do but warn us of what tangible things to expect."[16] James asserts that suffering and exhilaration are "belief-compelling"[17]—something which we can observe in both Crapsey's letters and the cinquain form. This proves equally true for some of Crapsey's Modernist contemporaries; we may consider James Joyce's eye troubles in summer 1918 and his struggle to finish *Ulysses*, or T.S. Eliot's self-diagnosed "nervous breakdown" in 1921, or Cyril Connolly's claim that disease, war, and death impose "unchanging limitations" on authors.[18]

But it is Virginia Woolf's lyrical essay, "On Being Ill" (1926), that best illuminates the perspectival shift caused by illness. As per the demands of its genre, "On Being Ill" commits a few romantic gestures to the page; for instance, Woolf calls the vast expanse of the ill person's intellect "[t]hat snowfield of the mind, where man has not trodden."[19] Nonetheless, Woolf bends figurative language to an accurate rendering of illness and its effects on the body and mind: she describe illness as "the waters of annihilation close above our heads."[20] For Woolf, ailments have been ignored or embellished in literature and criticism because, paradoxically, physical pain is a tactile—or "tangible," as James might put it— sensation that resists language. "[L]et a sufferer try to describe a pain in his head to a doctor," Woolf writes, "and language at once runs dry."[21]

Woolf proposes that illness requires "not only a new language

. . . , more primitive, more sensual, more obscene," but new fictional and poetic forms for exploring "a new hierarchy of the passions."[22] In some ways, the ill must shoulder the task of formal innovation; Woolf comments that the healthy and able-bodied, reminded of their own potential suffering, shy away from literary and actual sickbeds. Moreover, the healthy are rule-bound to social conventions and expectations. Only the ill, Woolf suggests, recognize modernity as an elaborate artifice, and only patients have the perspective necessary to deconstruct our attachment to schedules, occupations, and social commitments. Crapsey's letters and poems model Woolf's claim. Crapsey writes to Lowenthal that Smith College gossip "beguile[s] empty moments."[23] Similarly, her long-form poem, "To the Dead in the Grave-Yard Under My Window:—Written in A Moment of Exasperation," mocks the dead in an ironic indictment of the able-bodied: "I watch all night and not one ghost comes forth / To take its freedom of the midnight hour. / Oh, have you no rebellion in your bones?"[24]

But Crapsey, like Woolf, finds in illness a site of resistance. "But with the hook of life still in us," Woolf protests, "we must wriggle. We cannot stiffen peaceably into glassy mounds. Even the recumbent spring up at the mere imagination of frost about the toes and stretch out to avail themselves of the universal hope—Heaven, Immortality."[25] Even in the throes of sickness and on the verge of death, Woolf contends, the writer retains an ardent desire to create something that may, in time, jolt their readers, present and future.

The question, though, is *how* a writer can create in these circumstances. Woolf muses that fiction may not be up to the task: "Indeed it is to the poets that we turn. Illness makes us disinclined for the long campaigns that prose exacts." So the responsibility falls to poets, and it is a labor that Adelaide Crapsey performs in her invention of the cinquain.

4.

Every critique of Crapsey's work agrees on one point:

tuberculosis became the center of gravity during the last decade of her life. Crapsey's first biographer, Mary Elizabeth Osborn, remarks on "the mortal weariness which is so evident" in Crapsey's letters.[26] Smith situates the onset of Crapsey's tuberculosis at 1903, when the poet first suffered from chronic fatigue; from there, the brief account reads Crapsey's teaching career at Kemper Hall and Smith College, her efforts to research metrical patterns for *A Study in English Metrics*, and her poetry as fatal struggles against tuberculosis.[27] In 1979, Edmund Butscher notes that "her life and art were so visibly, so essentially intertwined," and that the worsening of her disease in 1910-11 accompanied her awakening as a poet and her development of the cinquain.[28] Even Crapsey's most recent biographer, Karen Alkalay-Gut, does not challenge this presumption: "it is now possible to perceive that Crapsey had organized her work in a form of sequence," Alkalay-Gut writes of *Verse*, "a progressive cumulative comprehension of the significance of death to literature and the writer."[29]

There is some debate over when Crapsey first started writing the compact, imagistic form that she called the "cinquain." Osborn dates the invention of the form at 1909, based on interviews with Crapsey's friends and colleagues.[30] Butscher suggests that the cinquains were composed primarily in 1911. Smith grapples with the extant archival evidence to better pinpoint the origins of the form, and she suggests that Crapsey's investigations into the history of metrical patterns planted the first seeds. Beginning in December 1908, Crapsey took a leave of absence from her teaching career and traveled to Europe, where she spent some time in Rome, Paris, London, and Kent. While in Europe, she read widely in short-form poetry, including haikus translated from the Japanese into French. While Smith expresses some dismay at Crapsey's European letters—it is a "disappointment," Smith says, that Crapsey never met or read Ezra Pound, H.D., or the other Imagists[31]—she nonetheless recognizes that Crapsey's encounter with Japanese literature, albeit in translation, likely provides a formal influence for the cinquain. The archive of Crapsey's papers seems to bear this out via three pages of transcriptions from Michel Revon's *Anthologie de la Littérature Japonaise*. Most striking is a translation (likely from a *French* translation) of "Lines—from the Japanese" by Yone Noguchi:

> I have cast the world
> And think one as nothing,
> Yet I feel cold on snow-falling day,
> And happy on flower-day.

Influence is an evasive beast, and the archive does not tell us to what extent Crapsey studied and practiced the conventions of Japanese short forms like the haiku and the tanka. Still, Crapsey's cinquains perform a similar tug between the forces of nostalgia and anticipation, enfeeblement and vitality. The melancholy of Noguchi's poem finds its twin in Crapsey's juxtaposition of winter and spring in "Arbutus": invoking the title's image of the evergreen plant, the speaker whispers that arbutus owes its vibrancy to winter's "faint breath" and "snows / rose-tinged."[32] (Indeed, Crapsey accomplishes in five lines a reversal that took Seamus Heaney thirteen lines in "The Haw Lantern.") The Noguchi poem's emotional swing from somber thought, to resignation, to uneasy hope further appears in Crapsey's "Fate Defied," when the speaker uses a simile to liken moonlight to a "mistily radiant" shroud.[33]

    This is one of the more conventional readings of the cinquain—as an Imagist riff on Japanese short-forms, a curious parallel evolution to Pound, H.D., and Amy Lowell's experiments. Yet, there is something unsatisfying about this argument, especially in the light of the frequent claim that Crapsey's poetics are inextricable from her biography. After all, there's the thesis of *A Study in English Metrics* to contend with: Crapsey's study of vocabulary and meter argues for viewing style and diction as the result of a poem's formal demands. During her travels in Europe, Crapsey performed much of the grueling labor—counting syllables, logging vocabulary in Milton, Tennyson, and so on—for *A Study in English Metrics*. It stands to reason that this labor would manifest in the cinquain's compact five lines. Indeed, the poem begins with a line of one iambic foot; the second line has two feet; the third has three feet; and the fourth has four feet, until the fifth line precipitously cuts to a terse, final foot.

Crapsey's devotion to English meter is not the only reason to complicate and recalibrate the influence-centric approach to the cinquain. The cinquain's brevity and terseness, its tight coupling of title and poetic content, and the dissonance between its honed imagery and cryptic minimalism—these align the form with Woolf's vision of a medium that accommodates the abilities of the ill writer, the reader's capacity to engage with disease, *and* what James might call the "tangible" bodily experience of tuberculosis. In her critique of tuberculosis as a literary trope, after all, Sontag reminds us that the diagnosis was "tantamount to hearing a sentence of death" and that "it was common to conceal the identity of their disease from tuberculars and, after they died, from their children";[34] Crapsey may have sought in the cinquain a form capable of capturing and communicating this warrant against her life.

Officially diagnosed with tuberculin meningitis in the summer of 1911, Crapsey's endurance would certainly have been compromised, and the question of mortality features heavily in the cinquains. While she was aware of her diagnosis, her case still entailed mystery and misdirection: she hid the diagnosis from her family for as long as possible, and Edward Baldwin—the trusted doctor tending her at Saranac Lake—often gave her a rosier prognosis, which she in turn shared through her letters.[35] In a 1929 memorandum, Baldwin recollects Crapsey's convalescence from September 1913 to August 1914:

> She was pathetic in her frailty and advanced invalidism, only fully realized after her arrival in the Adirondacks. She was rebellious at being obliged to give up her work at Smith College, but even more because of the disease she abhorred. It was obvious that she must be restricted in her desire to

continue work, yet almost at once she asked me questions as to her ability to do so, and finding a sympathetic attitude began to be cheerful and gather courage.[36]

It's difficult to say with any certainty if Crapsey found the cinquain's slight form to be a comfort while under Baldwin's care. Aside from some drafts and transcriptions, we unfortunately have little concrete evidence of her creative process. She seldom wrote of her poetry, and, as Osborn observes, some of Crapsey's intimates—most tellingly, her own mother—did not know that she was a poet until after her death.[37] Nonetheless, her letters speak to the vexations and exhaustion of writing criticism—a "long campaign," to borrow Woolf's line. In a May 1910 letter to her father, Crapsey says this of her research in the British Museum: "My work has gone not as fast as I hoped how[ev]er I hope to see where I am by the end of May . . . Every time I think of all the time that I wasted in College English departments I get a bit irritated."[38] Several weeks later, she apologizes to her parents for a "scrawly letter," in which she discusses *Modern Language Review*'s interest in her work on meter: "To tell the truth I've been working very hard and I'm pretty tired. This silly health of mine is most inconvenient."[39]

By 1913 and 1914, the last two years of her life, Crapsey's letters to Webster and Lowenthal turned more explicitly to her tuberculosis treatments. In October 1913, while convalescing at Saranac Lake, Crapsey pens this to Lowenthal: "Last week I did nothing but curse my fate—It would have made picturesque reading and I'm sorry I hadn't energy enough left to write it all down."[40] Less than a month later, she informs Lowenthal that "fresh and inexplicable weights of fatigue have settled down on me and my pen lags and drags."[41] In September 1914, back in her hometown of Rochester, Crapsey tries to treat her failing health with a bit of humor, when she writes to Webster: "Its [*sic*] funny how weak I am—I've never been so weak. Dear me troubles again!"[42]

5.

Even with Crapsey's letters at hand, any discussion of her creative process is naturally speculative. Still, the archive allows space to understand—to witness—the forces converging upon Crapsey as she developed and refined this poetic form: we know that Crapsey was unaware of the extent of her illness; we know that work on *A Study in English Metrics* exhausted her; we know that she developed the cinquain alongside her inquiries into meter and verse; and we also know that she persisted despite chronic fatigue and, later, Baldwin's irritation at "her desire to continue work."[43] To create poetry, Crapsey required a form that prioritized brevity. Moreover, the form needed to prove capable of altering perceptions, of imposing upon its reader the stasis, solitude, disruption, and wracking pains of the sickbed.

While we have no explicit evidence that Crapsey wrote cinquains *because* of tuberculosis, the cinquain's short form and its tendency to perturb the reader nonetheless cater to Woolf's demands on the literature of illness. "In illness, words seem to possess a mystic quality," Woolf reflects, "and the words give out their scent and distil their flavor, and then, if at last we grasp the meaning, it is all the richer for having come to us sensually first."[44] With only twenty-two syllables broken over five lines, the successful cinquain must operate according to a poetic version of Hemingway's iceberg principle: it must coldly and precisely supply only the most crucial sensory details, and yet leave an impression of a great mass beneath the surface.[45] Crapsey's "November Night" operates on the senses first, beginning with an invitation to the reader's ear:

> Listen. .
> With faint dry sound,
> Like steps of passing ghosts,
> The leaves, frost-crisp'd, break from the trees
> And fall.[46]

The poem's opening gesture—"Listen," with two periods that suggest something between a full stop and an ellipsis—asks the reader to huddle in toward the poem's speaker, like the famous *hwæt* that opens *Beowulf.* The poem then urges the reader to focus their hearing on the quality of the sound itself, a "faint dry sound" that suggests a processional of the dead. Only after the speaker alerts us to the sounds are we permitted to witness the source of the muffled noise: frozen leaves, the weight of ice just now breaking their stems.

"November Night" is, in a sense, the already dead haunting us with the illusion of life: dried leaves still present on their branches, a hushed and perhaps fearful speaker alerting the reader to the onset of winter and frost. Indeed, Crapsey stages many of her cinquains in the liminal space between late autumn and the first snowfalls, as if to impose on the reader (to riff on Wallace Stevens) a mind of winter. "Triad" lists "three silent things" associated with the cold, each of which is separated by Crapsey's signature two-thirds of an ellipsis: "the falling snow," "the hour / before dawn," and "the mouth of one / just dead."[47] Curiously, each of these items is silent, but only just: it is not hard to imagine the feather-stroke of a snowflake brushing either the cheek or a drift, or the birds about to awaken near the dawn, or the deceased's final exhalations. "Triad" is possessed by—or obsessed with—precarity, and signifies this through the wriggling tension of the double period. This in-between punctuation suggests a struggle to breath, but it is also a fluid grammatical sign somewhere between the trailing motion of an ellipsis (or falling snow) and the stiff finality of the period (or the "one just dead").[48]

The word "wriggle" feels apt in describing the sensation of reading Crapsey's most honed cinquains. "To wriggle" is, of course, Woolf's infinitive for the mental effort required of the sick artist, but the verb also suggests the wanderlust of reflection, the ill writhing in bedsheets, and the writer's tussle with language. The verb also conveys a dire sense of constraint, which Crapsey reports having felt in her classrooms at Smith College, English Department faculty meetings, the British Museum reading rooms, and her uneasy nights in Rome, Paris, and London. The sudden breaks in the lines and punctuation also suggest the troubled breathing that Crapsey would have experienced at the height of her illness at Saranac Lake. Such feelings may have manifested themselves in several of the cinquains, like "Moon-shadows" and its transmutation of "moon-cast shadows" on "windless nights" into the eventual stillness of "my heart when I am dead."[49] Similarly, "Trapped" smudges "day on day" together, compressing the hours into countless "weary year[s]" in its first four lines, before ending with a modern and nihilistically ironic "Well?"[50]

But the sense of eerie entrapment in Crapsey's cinquains feels most oppressive in pieces like "Niagara, Seen on a Night in November." In "Niagara," the speaker glances up to the sky (a perspective not so different from the patient recumbent in the sickbed) and focuses on the "frail. . .moon" suspended over the tumultuous falls. The skyward stare reduces the immense noise and furor of the Niagara, shifts the reader's attention away from a touristic fixation on the "crashing water," and evokes sympathy (if not concern) for the fragility of the moon. Here, as in "November Night," the implicit setting and engaged senses of the poem function like a double-exposure on a film negative: the speaker's glance toward the weak moon seems to superimpose itself over a more mundane experience, of turning our gaze from the panic and urgency of modernity to what only appears to be a distance, that gulf between the able-bodied person and the sickbed.

"Transformation transpires in a gaze," writes Donald Revell,[51] and in the cinquain, Crapsey focuses the reader's gaze on the twilit zones between sickness and health, autumn and winter, warmth and cold, light and dark. Not all of the cinquains succeed in effecting this change without sentimentalism; some are bogged with archaisms like "thee" and "thy," freighted biblical allusions, and other precious mannerisms drawn from Keats or Walter Savage Landor. But the most crystalline of Crapsey's cinquains suggest a writer employing those tools at hand—brevity, concision, and an intense knowledge of meter—to create a poetry representative of her bodily and psychological realities. It is no wonder that some of the most intimate cinquains select multivalent images that show the speaker's body sliding from health to sickness, or sickness to death. "Languor after Pain" suggests a brief awakening during a period of heavy sedation, during which the mind detaches from the body: "an opiate weariness / Settles on eye-lids, on relaxed / Pale wrists."[52] While the speaker of "Languor" doesn't register the sight of her own wrists, the voice in "Amaze" confides in the reader, making each of us sharers in the wistful recognition of how her hands (and, by association, our hands) wrinkle, crease, and become frailer with each successive year:

> I know
> Not these my hands
> And yet I think there was
> A woman like me once had hands
> Like these.[53]

6.

That a cinquain like "Amaze" can generate intimacy with, and evoke empathy from, its reader is emblematic not only of the form's power, but of poetry's. As Eliot suggests in "Tradition and the Individual Talent" (1919), poetry exists within the contexts of a specific moment, of a specific creative environment, but it has an indefinitely prolonged afterlife, in which its imagery and obsessions communicate with successive generations of readers and writers. The entwinement of Crapsey's cinquains with her medical history seem tailor-made for engaging twenty-first century readers navigating the ravages of chronic illness and the healthcare debates in the United States, Canada, and Great Britain.

But promoting this view is more difficult than charting Crapsey's poetic lineage. Her affection for Keats is well-documented; she wrote a poem entitled "John Keats" that imitates his style fluently; and there remains the aforementioned biographical fact, that both are too often read only through the prism of tuberculosis. Yet, in death, the looming presence of Keats, his poems, and his illness provide Crapsey with a touchstone, while illustrating how

Crapsey's work could function for readers in our moment. Writing her mother from Rome in 1909, Crapsey relates the story of a "funny thing" that occurred when she went to visit Keats' grave with Louise Merritt. "You know I'm not much of a person for doing things like that," Crapsey protests, in the same kittenish tone she would later adopt for describing her pneumothorax treatments to Lowenthal.[54] She then narrates the scene: she and Louise had gone to the wrong division of the cemetery, gotten themselves thoroughly lost, encountered an equally stranded man holding a clump of carnations, and struck up a conversation with that man. He was looking for the grave of an American academic—Milton scholar James Lee. They talked for some time of their poets, their fascinations, their respective family properties in Canandaigua. "Oh!" Crapsey exclaims, "then he knew who I was, and I knew who he was—his name was—Sherman Morse. Wasn't that odd?"[55]

Hardly so: poetry generates communities of readers, and using the poet's name as a metonym for her body of work provides us with a shorthand for striking up conversations with our peers. Moreover, a poet like Crapsey and her cinquain may provide us with our own means for writhing against the deleterious effects of physical and mental illness. The Scottish poet William Soutar borrowed Crapsey's invention during his own terminal bout with tuberculosis.[56] Bedridden in 1930, Soutar incorporated the cinquain in his sequence of short-form "epigrams," which wrestled with his failing health, the futility of medical interventions, and his own yearning to participate in the aesthetic and ideological agendas of Scottish Modernism. Comparing the poets, K.L. Goodwin states, "Pain and exhaustion probably dictated a characteristic brevity to both of them."[57] Indeed, like Crapsey's cinquains, Soutar's are Imagist poems that illustrate the body contending with its own frailties: Soutar's "Beyond Legend" rides the "surge. . .in our blood" and likens the "flesh" to "loam," while his poem "The Task" contends that the function of art is to represent "suffering and joy."[58]

Soutar is not alone in finding the cinquain an effective form for grappling with tuberculosis. Another such poet is Yvor Winters, who long championed Crapsey in verse anthologies and critical essays. In the introduction to his early poems, Winters recollects his diagnosis with tuberculosis in 1918, while he was a college student. From then until October 1921, Winters resided in a Santa Fé sanitarium to battle the disease. His voracious reading and tendency to craft what he called "experimental" poems mimics Crapsey's; indeed, he mentions having read Crapsey's *Verse* alongside Emily Dickinson and the Imagist poets.[59] In *Forms of Discovery* (1967), Winters interrupts his critique of innovations in short-form poetry to comment specifically on the link he feels to Crapsey's "predicament": "I know nothing of Miss Crapsey's medical history, but I know a great deal of my own, less than a decade later [than her illness] . . . The disease filled the body with a fatigue so heavy that it was an acute pain, pervasive and poisonous. Miss Crapsey must have known this fatigue, and most of her best work was written during the years of increasing illness."[60]

Soutar and Winters should not be alone in reading Crapsey's poetic innovations as a source of inspiration. With the West's discussions about improving mental health treatment, providing better access to recovery and treatment efforts, and securing medical care for all, the twenty-first century seems a prime moment to revisit Crapsey, her poetics, and the cinquain's intervention in the discourses of literature and medicine. Her poems could serve to stir empathy in readers unacquainted with the pain and suffering of chronic illness; furthermore, drawing critical and public attention to the cinquain may provide writers with a form capable of conveying not only a vantage point from the sickbed, but the physical and visceral sensations of living with illness. It falls on critics and poets alike to advocate for the cinquain and to nuance our reading of ill writers—so that we may better empathize with those who, like the speaker in Crapsey's "Release," feel a "pain [that] / Clanged back the doors that shut my soul / From life."[61]

NOTES

1 Adelaide Crapsey, Letter to Esther Lowenthal (4 February 1914), in *The Complete Poems and Collected Letters of Adelaide Crapsey*, ed. Susan Sutton Smith (Albany: State University of New York Press, 1977), 229. Unless noted otherwise, subsequent references to Crapsey's letters and individual poems cite the page numbers in Smith's *Complete Poems and Collected Letters*.

2 Ibid, 230.

3 Crapsey adopts a similar tone in her poem "Lines Addressed To My Left Lung Inconveniently Enamoured Of Plant-Life." Here, she directly addresses her lung and chastises it for "[a] freak I cannot pardon, / Thus to transform yourself into / A vegetable-garden" (119). The poem's meter is reminiscent of Gerard Manley Hopkins' use of sprung rhythm, while its manipulation of irony and slant rhyme anticipates Great War poets like Wilfred Owen and Siegfried Sassoon.

4 T.S. Eliot, "The Love Song of J. Alfred Prufrock," in *The Waste Land and Other Poems*, ed. Randy Malamud (New York: Barnes & Noble, 2005), 9.

5 Jean Webster, Commemoration of Adelaide Crapsey, in *Vassar Miscellany*. Reprinted as the preface in *Verse*, by Adelaide Crapsey (New York: Knopf, 1922), n.p.

6 Ibid, n.p.

7 Susan Sutton Smith, Introduction, in *The Complete Poems and Collected Letters of Adelaide Crapsey*, ed. Susan Sutton Smith (Albany: State University of New York Press, 1977), 23.

8 Claude Bragdon, Foreword, in *Verse*, by Adelaide Crapsey (New York: Knopf, 1922), n.p.

9 Crapsey, "Shadow," 75.

10 The reviews cited here, along with others, are archived in Adelaide Crapsey's papers at the University of Rochester.

11 Yvor Winters, *In Defense of Reason* (Denver: Swallow Press-University of Denver Press, 1947), 568.

12 Jean Mason, "Tuberculosis as Muse: Three Poets on North America's Magic Mountain," *Ars Medica: Journal of Medicine, the Arts, and the Humanities* 1, no. 1 (2004): 28-29.

13 Edmund Wilson, "The Wound and the Bow," in *The Wound and the Bow: Seven Studies in Literature* (New York: Farrar, Straus & Giroux, 1978), 235.

14 Lionel Trilling, "Freud and Imagination," in *The Liberal Imagination: Essays on Literature and Society* (New York: New York Review Books, 2008), 42.

15 Lionel Trilling, "Art and Neurosis," in *The Liberal Imagination: Essays on Literature and Society* (New York: New York Review Books, 2008), 164-5.

16 William James, *The Principles of Psychology*, vol. 2 (New York: Henry Holt & Co.-Dover Press, 1950), 306. James is not entirely innocent of the error that Bragdon, Wilson, Trilling, and others would later make: the first volume of

his *Principles of Psychology* reflects on the "mutations of the self" that occur as a consequence of bodily and mental illness.

17 Ibid, 306, 307.

18 Cyril Connolly, *Enemies of Promise* (New York: Persea, 1983), 135. Here, though, Connolly cannot restrain himself from sarcastically remarking on London readers' expectations that the creative temperament and poor health are inseparable: "The health of a writer should not be too good, and perfect only in those periods of convalescence when he is not writing."

19 Virginia Woolf, "On Being Ill," ed. Hermione Lee (Ashfield: Paris Press, 2002), 15-16.

20 Ibid, 3.

21 Ibid, 7.

22 Ibid.

23 Crapsey, Letter to Ester Lowenthal (25 September 1913), 210.

24 Crapsey, "To the Dead in the Grave-Yard Under My Window:—Written in A Moment of Exasperation," 101.

25 Woolf, "On Being Ill," 17.

26 Mary Elizabeth Osborn, *Adelaide Crapsey* (Boston: Bruce Humphries, 1933), 49.

27 Smith, Introduction, 4.

28 Edmund Butscher, *Adelaide Crapsey* (Boston: Twayne, 1979), 16, 54.

29 Karen Alkalay-Gut, "Death, Order, and Poetry: The 'Presentation Copy ' of Adelaide Crapsey," *American Literature* 57, no. 2 (1985): 264.

30 See Osborn, *Adelaide Crapsey*, 40. Curiously, Osborn undercuts this point with a stroke of novelistic embellishment about a 1908 visit which Crapsey paid to Niagara Falls with her friend, one Miss Pritchard: Osborn suggests, without any archival evidence, that the cinquain "Niagara, Seen on a Night in November" was written directly after the trip with Pritchard.

31 Smith, Introduction, 10.

32 Crapsey, "Arbutus," 74.

33 Crapsey, "Arbutus," 75.

34 Susan Sontag, *Illness and Its Metaphors*, in *Susan Sontag: Essays of the 1960s and '70s* (New York: Library of America-Farrar, Straus & Giroux, 2013), 678.

35 Butscher, *Adelaid Crapsey*, 21-22.

36 Edward Baldwin, "Adelaide Crapsey – 1913," Box 1, Folder 2, A.C89, Adelaide Crapsey Papers (Rochester: University of Rochester, 13 September 2017). Baldwin misstates several facts in the course of his memorandum. The transcript claims that Crapsey left Saranac Lake in March 1914. This is crossed out in pencil, with the correct date of her departure (September 1914) written in its place.

37 Osborn, *Adelaide Crapsey*, 8.

38 Crapsey, Letter to Algernon Crapsey (May 1910), 192.

39 Crapsey, Letter to Algernon Crapsey (24 May 1910), 195.

40 Crapsey, Letter to Esther Lowenthal (15 October 1913), 213.

41 Crapsey, Letter to Esther Lowenthal (6 November 1913), 216.

42 Crapsey, Letter to Jean Webster (19 September 2014), 203.

43 Baldwin, "Adelaide Crapsey – 1913," 1.

44 Woolf, "On Being Ill," 20-21.

45 See Ernest Hemingway, *Death in the Afternoon* (London: Vintage Books, 2000), 169.

46 Crapsey, "November Night," 70.

47 Crapsey, "Triad," 70.

48 Crapsey's use of unusual punctuation suggests a space for further critical interventions. In the editions of *Verse* published shortly after her death, the editors imposed on the poems a strict and more conventional use of periods and ellipses; the *Complete Poems and Collected Letters* restores the punctuation to those used in Crapsey's manuscript copies. Moreover, Crapsey is not alone in her compelling use of the double period: Jean Toomer's *Cane* also makes use of this evocative, nontraditional punctuation. I am grateful to my colleague Sheila Liming for pointing me toward Toomer's use of the double period.

49 Crapsey, "Moon-shadows," 71.

50 Crapsey, "Trapped," 71. Even though she invented the cinquain, Crapsey obviously intends for the cinquain to allow some measure of expressive freedom: the final "Well?" in "Trapped" comprises the poem's entire final line, meaning that Crapsey purposefully broke the poem's final iambic foot.

51 Donald Revell, *The Art of Attention: A Poet's Eye* (Minneapolis: Graywolf, 2007), 45.

52 Crapsey, "Languor after Pain," 72.

53 Crapsey, "Amaze," 75.

54 Crapsey, Letter to Adelaide T. Crapsey (1909), 179.

55 Ibid.

56 K.L. Goodwin notes that Hugh MacDiarmid, a central figure in Scottish poetry, described Soutar in much the same vein that Bragdon described Crapsey: "Despite the fact that he was bedfast for many years," MacDiarmid declaims, "his demeanour generally evoked tributes to his amazing serenity of spirit, the fineness of his character, and his freedom from the slightest trace of rancour or repining" (MacDiarmid qtd. in Goodwin, "William Soutar," 97).

57 K.L. Goodwin, "William Soutar, Adelaide Crapsey, and Imagism," *Studies in Scottish Literature* 3, no. 2 (1965): 98.

58 William Soutar, "Beyond Legend" and "The Task," in *Poems of William Soutar: A New Selection*, ed. W.R. Aitken (Edinburgh: Scottish Academic Press, 1988), 70, 69.

59 Yvor Winters, "Introduction to *The Early Poems*," in *Yvor Winters: Uncollected Essays and Reviews*, ed. Francis Murphy (Chicago: Swallow Press, 1973), 310-12.

60 Yvor Winters, *Forms of Discovery: Critical and Historical Essays on the Forms of the Short Poem in English* (Denver: Alan Swallow, 1967), 329.

61 Crapsey, "Release," 70.

BIBLIOGRAPHY

Alkalay-Gut, Karen. *Alone in the Dawn: The Life of Adelaide Crapsey*. Athens: University of Georgia Press, 1988.

———. "Death, Order, and Poetry: The 'Presentation Copy' of Adelaide Crapsey." *American Literature* 57, no. 2 (1985): 263-289. JSTOR.

Baldwin, Edward. "Adelaide Crapsey – 1913." (Memorandum on Crapsey's condition at Saranac Lake.) Box 1, Folder 2. A.C89. Adelaide Crapsey Papers, University of Rochester. Rochester, NY. 13 Sept. 2017.

Bragdon, Claude. Foreword. In *Verse*, by Adelaide Crapsey, n.p. New York: Alfred A. Knopf, 1922.

Butscher, Edmund. *Adelaide Crapsey*. Boston: Twayne, 1979.

Connolly, Cyril. *Enemies of Promise*. 1938. New York: Persea, 1983.

Crapsey, Adelaide. *Verse*. New York: Alfred A. Knopf, 1922.

Crapsey, Adelaide. *The Complete Poems and Collected Letters of Adelaide Crapsey*, edited by Susan Sutton Smith. Albany: SUNY Press, 1977.

Eliot, T.S. "The Love Song of J. Alfred Prufrock." In *The Waste Land and Other Poems*, edited Randy Malamud, 9-13. New York: Barnes & Noble, 2005.

Goodwin, K.L. "William Soutar, Adelaide Crapsey, and Imagism." *Studies in Scottish Literature* 3, no. 2 (1965): 96-100. Scottish Literature Collections at Scholar Commons.

Hemingway, Ernest. *Death in the Afternoon*. 1932. London: Penguin-Vintage Classics, 2000.

James, William. *The Principles of Psychology*. 1890. Vol. 2. New York: Henry Holt & Co.-Dover, 1950.

Jones, Llewelyn. "A First and Last Book." Rev. of *Verse* by Adelaide Crapsey. In *New Republic*. Box 1, Folder 11. A.C89. Adelaide Crapsey Papers, University of Rochster. Rochester, NY. 13 Sept. 2017.

Joyce, James. *Letters of James Joyce*, edited by Stuart Gilbert. New York: Viking, 1957.

Mason, Jean. "Tuberculosis as Muse: Three Poets on North America's Magic Mountain." *Ars Medica: Journal of Medicine, the Arts, and the Humanities* 1, no. 1 (2004): 23-30. Box 4, Folder 18. A.C89. Adelaide Crapsey Papers, University of Rochester. Rochester, NY. 14 Sept. 2017.

Noguchi, Yone. "Lines—from the Japanese." Translated from French by Adelaide Crapsey. Box 2, Folder 6. A.C89. Adelaide Crapsey Papers, University of Rochester. Rochester, NY. 13 Sept. 2017.

Osborn, Mary Elizabeth. *Adelaide Crapsey*. Boston: Bruce Humphries, 1933.

Rev. of *Verse* by Adelaide Crapsey. In *Boston Transcript*. Box 4, Folder 14. A.C89. Adelaide Crapsey Papers, University of Rochester. Rochester, NY. 14 Sept. 2017.

Rev. of *Verse* by Adelaide Crapsey. *Book of the Week*. Box 1, Folder 11. A.C89. Adelaide Crapsey Papers, University of Rochester. Rochester, NY. 13 Sept. 2017.

Revell, Donald. *The Art of Attention: A Poet's Eye*. Minneapolis: Graywolf, 2007.

Smith, Susan Sutton. Introduction. In *The Complete Poems and Collected Letters of Adelaide Crapsey*, edited by Susan Sutton Smith, 1-58. Albany: State University of New York Press, 1977.

Sontag, Susan. *Illness and Its Metaphors*. In *Susan Sontag: Essays of the 1960s and '70s*, 675-729. New York: Library of America-Farrar, Straus & Giroux, 2013.

Soutar, William. *Poems of William Soutar: A New Selection*, edited by W.R. Aitken. Edinburgh: Scottish Academic P, 1988.

Trilling, Lionel. "Art and Neurosis." In *The Liberal Imagination*, 160-180. New York: New York Review Books, 2008.

———. "Freud and Literature." In *The Liberal Imagination*, 34-57. New York: New York Review Books, 2008.

Webster, Jean. Preface. In *Verse*, by Adelaide Crapsey, n.p. New York: Alfred A. Knopf, 1922.

Wilson, Edmund. "The Wound and the Bow." In *The Wound and the Bow: Seven Studies in Literature*, 223-242. New York: Farrar, Straus & Giroux, 1978.

Winters, Yvor. *Forms of Discovery: Critical and Historical Essays on the Forms of the Short Poem in English*. Denver: Alan Swallow, 1967.

———. *In Defense of Reason*. Denver: Swallow Press-University of Denver Press, 1947.

———. "Introduction to *The Early Poems*." 1966. *Yvor Winters: Uncollected Essays and Reviews*, edited by Francis Murphy, 310-316. Chicago: Swallow Press, 1973.

Woolf, Virginia. "On Being Ill," edited and with an introduction by Hermione Lee. Ashfield: Paris Press, 2002.

EDITORS' NOTES & ACKNOWLEDGEMENTS

EDITORS' NOTES

JENNY MOLBERG is the author of *Marvels of the Invisible*, which won the 2014 Berkshire Prize (Tupelo Press, 2017). She is the recipient of a scholarship from the Sewanee Writers Conference and a fellowship from Vermont Studio Center. Her poems have appeared in *Best New Poets, Poetry International, Ploughshares, Boulevard, Green Mountains Review, The Missouri Review*, and other publications. She is assistant professor of creative writing at the University of Central Missouri, where she co-edits *Pleiades*.

CHRISTIAN BANCROFT is the recipient of a Michener Fellowship. His work has appeared or is forthcoming in *Callaloo, The Missouri Review, jubilat*, and *Asymptote*, among others. He is currently a PhD Candidate at the University of Houston, where he is working on a book about queering translation, and has completed a poetry manuscript on the persecution of queer men and women during the Holocaust.

ACKNOWLEDGEMENTS

From Jenny Molberg: Many thanks to Kevin Prufer and Wayne Miller, and the Unsung Masters Series Board for making this project possible: Sarah Ehlers, Ben Johnson, Sally Connolly, and Joanna Luloff. Kevin, thank you so much for your enthusiasm about Adelaide Crapsey and your invaluable guidance. Kate Nuernberger, thank you for your advice, hard work, dedication to Pleiades Press, and most importantly, your friendship. Thank you to the University of Rochester Library, and their help with this collection. I am enormously grateful to the English Department at the University of Houston, and their anonymous donor, without whom this project would not be possible. This project was also made possible by the English Department at the University of Central Missouri and the College of Arts and Social Sciences—thanks especially to Dr. Dan Schierenbeck, Chair of the English Department. Thanks to Ben Johnson for your guidance and support, and for many converations about Crapsey during our commute. A thousand thanks to all the scholars and poets who provided essays and blurbs for this collection—we could not have done this without you. Christian, I owe you an enormous debt of gratitude. Thank you for your tireless work and dedication to research, for believing in Crapsey and in me, for your patience, and for your tenacity. Finally, thank you to my grandmother, Sue Deakins, for teaching me about the millions of worlds that can live on a bookshelf, and that boredom is only for those without imaginations. You and Adelaide would have been great friends.

From Christian Bancroft: First, Kevin Prufer, Wayne Miller, and those who gave me the opportunity to work on this project. Thank you. Of course, all of our contributors must be thanked profusely for their excellent work in this issue. The book wouldn't be what it is without them. Again, Kevin and Kate for offering their support and editorial acumen as Jenny and I encountered issues throughout the creation of this volume. Sally Connolly, who also offered her support and wisdom to me when I had questions. The Unsung Masters Board Members for all of their hard work and support. J, the English Department at UH, and an anonymous donor for providing the funds necessary for me to take a trip to the archives. The book could not have been completed without that trip. Everyone at Rare Books, Special Collections and Preservation at the University of Rochester who helped Jenny and me. Most importantly, Melinda Wallington, Phyllis Andrews, and the undergraduate staff at the library, who were of great help to me during my trip to the archives. Robin Crapsey Romero must also be thanked, for her unwavering support of this project and for allowing Jenny and me to use whatever materials of Crapsey's required for the book. I also must thank Jenny for everything that she's done to ferry this project to completion. Jenny, thank you thank you thank you, for all of your hard work, dedication, support, wisdom, guidance, and ten thousand other descriptive words that I could use to describe your help on this Unsung Masters issue. I had no idea how fabulous it was going to be to have the opportunity to work with you. Finally, Adrienne Perry, for her love and her own editorial guidance on this book. You were always there when I had some concern—big or small—about the book, and what's more, you were always happy to help me out. You are my lodestar.

This book is produced as a collaboration
between the Departments of English
at University of Central Missouri
and University of Houston.

GENEROUS SUPPORT AND FUNDING PROVIDED BY:

Houston Arts Alliance
University of Houston
Missouri Arts Council
University of Central Missouri
National Endowment for the Arts

and

An anonymous donor to the University of Houston's
Department of English who is committed to offering
talented graduate students with opportunities
to develop their critical and research skills.

This book is set in Adobe Caslon Pro type
with Dense titles.

Designed by Martin Rock.
Typeset by Jenny Molberg & Martin Rock.